BEST OF TEMP S

BEST OF TEMP SLAVE!

WISCONSIN STATE JOURNAL

Terrorism
hits the
heartland!
TEMP SLAVE! ZINE

The

T
Cap
Tim

PHOTO BY CELISA DICKSON

edited by Jeff Kelly.

Garrett County Press

For information address
Garrett County Press, PO Box 896, Madison, WI 53701.
www.gcpress.com

⊜ GCPress books are printed on acid-free paper.

Text Designed by Alice Gail Carter & Pete Sickman-Garner

LIBRARY OF CONGRESS CATALOG CARD NUMBER: 97-75103

ISBN 1-891053-42-6

First Edition—1997

ACKNOWLEDGEMENTS

A publishing project can not succeed without the help of others. The following people gave their support, advice, and friendship over the past five years. Some of them even sent me money.

Alvin at Pic A Books, Jen Angel, Ann of Bottle Fed zine, Judi Bari, Beanie, Brendan Bartholomew, Doug Biggert, Bonnie Burton, Clay Butler, Chloe and Reading Frenzy, Marci Davis, Gloria Diaz, Dishwasher Pete, Big Bill Dunham, Miranda Edison and Black Out Books, Seth Friedman and Factsheet Five, Joshua Glenn, Jim and Debbie Goad, David Hirshi and Desert Moon, Kenny the Carny, Linda, Russell, Matthew and Left Bank Books, Lumpen, Dave McGurgan, Jason McQuinn, Jennifer Phistry, Ramsey and AK Press, Marcia and the Rainbow Bookstore, Melissa Roberts, Maureen Shea, Peter Sickman-Garner, Steve and Sherrie Syvmbersky, Swiss Chris, Tom and the Bound Together Collective, UAW Solidarity Magazine.

Finally, a big thanks and pat on the back to G.K. Darby who made this book possible!

INTRODUCTION

Something wasn't right.

It was late December in 1994, and my boss was telling me that I was going to lose my job in two weeks. For the previous year I had worked in a mailroom at a regional office of a large international insurance company. I had started as a temp, and had been promised full time employment. The boss man was now telling me otherwise.

This was my introduction to the brave new corporate future of the disposable workforce.

America, one of the world's richest countries, has decided that the social pact between employer and employee is no longer relevant. There are no guarantees. The party is over. The crashing thud of expectations and hopes have come tumbling down like a decrepit building caught in a strong wind.

When a single person loses a job or is forced to temp for a living, it's a problem. When the *New York Times* announces that the largest single employer in the United States is Manpower Temps, well then, you're talking about millions of employees and millions of problems.

Temporary work is a strong after effect of corporate downsizing, micro-management, and the trend toward specialization. With a straight face, temp agencies can advertise the fact that they employ temp surgeons, accountants, computer programmers, teachers. Every single occupation is under the gun. Estimates run the gamut between 2 to 30 million people who are considered contingent workers, part timers, contract workers, or temp workers. There is no end in sight either, experts have commented on the possibility of half the working population becoming temp workers within the next 20 years.

The explosion of temp work has also been ushered in by the weakness of a diminished labor movement, unsure of itself after a decade of defeats at the hands of corporados. Starting with the fiasco of the Air Traffic Contoller strike in 1981, during which close to 15,000 federal employees were summarily fired by the Reagan administration, labor has seen its power and influence wane in the face of a full fledged attack on worker rights. Into this void comes the temporary agency. Business wants nothing to do with the maintenance of its workforce. Thus, an industry that once operated in the shadows has evolved into a major player on the corporate scene. The pact is no longer between worker and employer, rather, it's between employer and middleman in the form of the temp agency.

As such, a growing population of working people meanders through life moving from job to job, with no benefits and no feeling of belonging. When the smiley faced articles are written about the joys of temping, you're more likely to be told about flexibility, freedom, and skill specialization. Not the percentage paid to temp agencies. Not the mental and financial stress faced by temp workers on a daily basis. For instance, what will temp workers retire on when their work lives come to an end? Youth is fleeting. Eventually the price bargained for in the present will have to be paid in the future.

I'm reminded of a situation described in a Hunter S. Thompson book on the Hells Angels. Thompson watches as some young kids walk over to a biker and compliment him on his motorcycle. The biker relies, "Thanks, it's all I got." For most Americans, their job is all they got. It's how they plan for the future. It's how they describe themselves. For better or worse, work, or a job, is a meaningful measure of worthiness. If this is in fact the case, then there are millions of people feeling despondent because what pray tell can they offer as an explanation regarding their occupation? "I'm a temp worker," just doesn't seem to cut it.

American corporations are playing a tricky game right now. They are betting the bank that working people will overlook the scenario and accept temp work as a reality. Anomie, isolation, disillusionment work best within small disconnected groups or individuals. Working people tend to focus blame solely on themselves for their economic situation. However, the isolation falls away when people of similar circumstances begin to recognize shared interests and career paths. This shared recognition is the beginning of the formation of a consciousness. The formation of consciousness is the first important step leading to action.

Without a true understanding of the prevailing employment situation at the time, and with little or no expectations about who would actually read *Temp Slave!* the first issue was produced in the last two weeks of my employment at an insurance company. It was meant as a personal documentation of my own frustrations. The zine quickly grew to include other voices and became known in alternative publishing circles, and then began reaching a more mainstream audience. Over the course of five years, the circulation of *Temp Slave!* has grown from 25 readers to 3000 or more readers. To my surprise, the zine even developed an international readership. Subscription and contributor driven, there were never any paid ads to support the project. The zine succeeded because, like the temp agencies, it filled a void for the kind of working people who were frustrated enough to put into words their frustration with their work lives.

This is an unusual book. The stories within the pages of this book best reflect the hopes and emotions of its authors. But, you have to have an open mind: these stories do not comprise a seamless thread. Bosses and temp agencies bear the brunt of temp worker rage, but, being a temp allows the worker an inside view of workplace politics. So naturally there are plenty of comments about the soulless, robotic worker drones who carry out the everyday mundane tasks that keep the wheels of business turning. In many cases, a coworker is not a comrade, he's an enemy. After all, in most work places, many regular workers look at temps as a threat to their own jobs.

Although many of the writers are educated, their viewpoints are not written from a journalistic or academic perspective. They are not outsiders to the issue; rather, they are active participants with a first person view of the situation at hand. Some of the writers support the labor movement. Others would laugh in your face if you even said the word "union." Many of the writers actually enjoy work and only hope for a regular full time job. Still others want nothing to do with being a "good citizen" and living off of corporate handouts. They are more likely to sabotage their bosses, or blow the whistle on corporate malfeasance by publicly exposing the darker side of corporate life. A fair description of *Temp Slave!* is that it follows in the tradition of oral history. Most history, most news that is reported covers the accomplishments of the elites, whether they be corporate raiders, or politicians. *Temp Slave!* turns this upside down and reports on people who actually work for a living. You can agree or disagree with the writers. No matter, the writing comes from the gut, the street level of personal experience.

While *Temp Slave!* is a labor-oriented publication with a political bent, it doesn't tow the line regarding the various competing orthodoxies. Unlike a lot of other publications, there is great humor to be found in the pages of *Temp Slave!* Some of the best cartoonists in America were featured. My contribution to the zine was a combination of writing, cartooning and editing. Fearful of being blackballed by employers, I wrote my stories under the alias "Keffo." This gave me room to explore my own demons in front of a sometimes bewildered but always amused readership.

The greatest compliment any publication can receive is strong critical reaction, media attention and passionate readers. If you express viewpoints counter to prevalent thought then you can expect disapproval of your work. Countless readers, some of whom were temp agency hacks, denounced the ideas within *Temp Slave!* Some thought it extreme. Others made light of what they termed the continual "whining" expressed by contributors. My only reply was to reinforce that the so called "whiners" had every right to express their displeasure. After all, just because you're being forced to eat a shit sandwich doesn't mean you have to like it too.

On the other hand, the media focus on *Temp Slave!* has been heavy, almost every single mainstream media source including the *New York Times, Wall Street Journal, US News and World Report, USA Today, CBS News, Wired, NPR,* and others have contacted me regarding interviews and information about the burgeoning temp agency growth. All this for a little zine produced and written on an old computer located in a messy bedroom.

Most important were the *Temp Slave!* readers who became like a second family to me. Letters from readers and contributions described what seemed like a diaspora of individuals untethered to their jobs, with no real hopes for the future. *Temp Slave!* as a publication could do nothing to alleviate the situation. It did and will continue to allow people space to say what they want. It served and will serve as a central meeting point for disaffected workers. It opened up debate for divergent points of view. For these reasons alone, I am justly proud of the contributions *Temp Slave!* made on the issues of work life in 1990's America.

This book is dedicated to all the working people out there struggling for a better life.

JEFF KELLY

TABLE OF CONTENTS

WORK!

THE JOB OF THE NINETIES

Unless you have specialized training you will have to go to a temporary service for a job. Temporary job services are the middlemen in the worker-for-hire industry. No matter which agency you work for, no matter where you live, if you are a temporary worker you are getting ripped off.

The scam goes like this.

A temp agency charges a company a certain rate, say $10 an hour and the worker gets paid maybe $6 an hour. This is a sweet deal because on one hand the agency makes $4 an hour on every worker. On the other hand the company does not have to deal with benefits, nor does it have to care about employee relations since a temp employee can easily be replaced with another temp.

This never ending treadmill of low pay, no benefits, no security and no respect means that the temp worker is nothing but a body, a body to be sacrificed to the whims and wishes of a corporate mentality gone berserk. It is greed and greed alone that creates this situation.

The funny (or not so funny) part is that temp agencies and corporations actually want you to believe that they like you. They want you to believe this because without a semblance of loyalty — arriving on time, doing the boring work, accepting the abuse, they can both go merrily on their ways making piles of money. So do not be fooled by the smiling faces or assurances that you will become a full time employee, because the smiling face hides a dagger and the assurances are lies.

Temp workers are not only used for cheap labor, they are used to keep full timers in line. Temps are used to make full timers think twice about raising questions about work conditions since the threat of replacement by a temp is all the more possible. Full timers have a name for temps — "Job Snatchers." To a certain degree the paranoid full timer is correct but basically temps and full timers want the same things. Mostly, a pressure free job that pays a decent salary and benefits. Corporate bosses (corporados) do not want this, however they want work done at a fast pace for little pay and no benefits and anything that makes this possible is positive. If a full timer doesn't like the job, fine, they can be fired. If a temp doesn't like the job they can be replaced with another temp.

In 1990's America no job is safe and no temp worker should believe they will get a full time job through hard work. Bosses in the 1990's want you to stay in place, keep you down and take advantage of your work.

Therefore, there is no reason whatsoever for a temp to have any loyalty for a company. In the 1990's, American corporations are upgrading their technology, downsizing their workforce or moving operations to low wage countries like Mexico.

So having said all this, why do people accept temporary work? First, let's dispel a lie. Temp agency bro-chures show smiling faces of happy workers. But the fact is, temp workers don't like being temp workers one bit. Some people though take temp jobs to pay for Christmas, a vacation or to keep themselves busy. BUT the vast majority do it to survive — to pay bills, put food on the table and take care of their children. BUT we are not doing well, are we? We are not doing well because the rich men who run the corporations will not let us do well and they will never let us do well.

So do these rich assholes deserve loyalty? Hell no! What they deserve is a kick in the ass. Would you like to learn how to kick them in the ass? Read on. The following stories, comics and information are written by temps to show you that you are not alone.

KEFFO

The Boss

DEFINITIONS OF THE WORD:

BUSINESSMAN!

1 A tricky or worthless person: a scamp.

2 A low, contemptible fellow; a scoundrel.

3 The great enemy of humanity and of goodness, extremely malicious or wicked.

4 Gluttonous, voracious, avaricious, piggish, insatiable

5 A mentally deficient person.

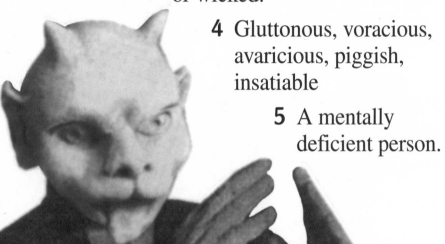

OOPS! I'm sorry. I mistakenly looked up the definitions of:
scalawag, scab, Satan, greedy, and imbecile
and substituted it for the definition of Businessman.
Oh hell, it's all the same anyway!   — KEFFO

Why Bosses Are Assholes

"I hate this fucking place and I'm looking for another job." Sounds like a temp worker, but it isn't — this is what my boss said to me while I was temping. As temp workers, we are at the bottom of the barrel. However, the bosses that we deal with directly are not far removed from our own situation. Lower and middle managers are the people on the bubble, people most likely to eat a shit sandwich from their superiors. In fact, these managers are an endangered species because corporate America is pulling the rug out from under them. All across America, managers are heading to the unemployment line. College grads from the most prestigious schools are finding it next to impossible to gain entry into the halls of coprodumb. It almost breaks my heart.

I cannot in good conscience feel sorry for these people, because it is managers who maintain the whole rotten system. They are much like the clean fingered technicians who perpetuate the war economy without seeing the end result of their product. However, I can fully understand why these people are assholes. Let me bend your ear.

Your boss has just returned from a production review meeting shaking his head and mumbling to himself. He's just been told by the higher ups that he has to cut his workforce and increase output at the same time. This poses some problems for the boss. On one hand, his employees are low paid and morale is low. How does he wring more production out of full timers and temps? He can't really. So now he's in big time

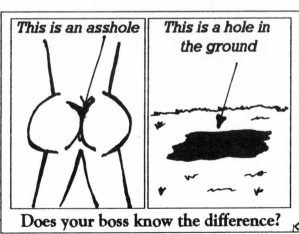

This is an asshole | **This is a hole in the ground**

Does your boss know the difference?

3

Mirror, Mirror on the wall, whose the fairest boss of . . .

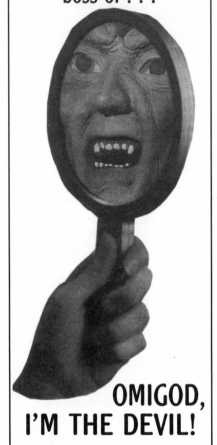

OMIGOD, I'M THE DEVIL!

KEFFO

shit. He's caught between a hostile workforce and a hostile upper management. He either gets the job done or he can kiss any future aspirations goodbye.

How motivated your boss is to go along and get along will determine what kind of boss he is. From my experiences the boss usually takes the asshole route — he becomes overbearing. Think about it, bosses, especially managers are not creative types. If the nipple (the company) was pulled away from them, they would cry. Their job is their whole identity. Thus bosses are assholes.

No matter how you cut it, we as temps have nothing in common with these people.

Certainly, not in the workplace where our interests are different. For example, I for one want the same kind of respect from people that I give them. This is not possible in the hierarchial system of most companies. In fact my boss continually used the term "My people" when referring to his employees. This to me smacks of a slave/master relationship. Nor are there any grounds outside of work. Much like racists, bosses cannot escape the ignorance of their lives. There is always a barrier to be maintained. I've been around these people and they are almost horrified to learn that I have other interests, that I have a mind. This scares them because they equate intelligence with your position on the corporate ladder.

One time I listened in on a conversation between two friends over whether or not we needed police. The argument ended abruptly when one said to the other, "OK you like the police, well, would you go out for a drink with a cop?" Well, now I have to ask, "Would you go out to drink with your boss?" If you did, what would you say to him? Maybe you would get piss drunk and tell him how much you like to sabotage your work area. That would sure score you some points!

Summing it all up, bosses are assholes because they

are repressed. Despite a front that says, "Our company is progressive, gets the job done etc ..." the reality is that corporations and bosses succeed only by luck, sometimes by expertise, but seldom if ever through team work.

Take a good look at your boss. He's an asshole, but he too has a noose around his neck. And he knows it.

KEFFO

Murder in the Workplace!

Surprise surprise. One of the leading causes of death throughout the past few years is murder in the workplace. At an alarming rate, disgruntled workers are beginning to run amok, causing murder and mayhem on the job. Usually, a worker gets fired and then goes to a gun shop, buys a gun and returns to work and shoots up the place, taking revenge on bosses and coworkers.

For some strange reason, postal workers seem to be the people most likely to snap, followed very closely by office clerical workers. The one thing that both groups of workers have in common is that they are forced to do mind numbing paper work day after day. Usually their supervisors are slave drivers and usually the murderous worker has been passed over for a promotion.

Easy access to hand guns and automatic weapons has made it possible for almost anyone to acquire a gun legally. If a weapon can not be acquired legally, it is even easier to acquire a "Saturday Night Special" on the black market. Guns, mixed with frustration in the workplace means that a heavy price might be paid by an innocent bystander.

Seeing that many full time workers are crazy to begin with, temps should do whatever is possible to maintain their safety. After all, it makes sense to want to walk out the front door of the building you work in rather than to be carried out in a body bag. Here are a few tips to protect

BOSSES ARE IDIOT

5

yourself.

1 Know where all the emergency exists are.

2 Find out if the building you work in has a security system — either guards or access keys and pads. If not ask that the company install one.

3 If you work with someone showing high levels of stress ask if you can be placed elsewhere.

4 Avoid working in one door rooms.

5 Do not insult or egg on a worker who is visibly upset about a work related problem. This can lead to serious consequences!

Being a temp in itself is a very frustrating, somewhat depressing situation. Many temps never know where they will be working from week to week or even day to day. This situation can cause horrible financial and psychological problems. However, there is no reason to go off your nut, pick up a gun and initiate target practice on other human beings. As mentioned throughout this mini-zine, there are other, more fun ways at getting back at the slave drivers.

However, if you do lose your mind and snap out please remember a few things.

1 Do not shoot your coworkers. They are probably as frustrated as you and just because they don't want to shoot people doesn't make them bad people.

2 Do not shoot full timers. Well at least know the difference between a bad one and a good one.

3 If you must murder someone, please make sure that it is a boss. Bosses usually wear white shirts, ties, shiny shoes and carry brief cases. Identify and know who your bosses are.

4 Start at the top. Go for the President of the company first and work your way down.

5 Finally! Whatever you do, don't shoot me!

KEFFO

THE HIDDEN MEANING OF CORPORATE LOGOS!

WE FUCK WITH YOU

WE'RE ALL BULLSHIT

WE ARE ALWAYS WATCHING YOU

BOSSES ARE ASSHOLES

TREADMILL

CORPORATE PEOPLE ARE CLOWNS

SMILE! YOU ARE BEING ZAPPED BY RADIATION

Blood! Blood! Blood!

I was thrilled to learn that the TV show *48 Hours* would be running an hour long story on "Terror on the Job." I sat back in my easy chair, popped open a beer and anxiously awaited the show to begin.

In typical fashion, CBS sent clueless reporters to interview people whose family members had been killed by workers run amok. Their wide-eyed looks and stupid questions caused me to laugh out loud. I still for the life of me cannot understand how the major networks are able to stay in business. Still, it does make for bad "good" TV.

Anyway, the show detailed some recent murders in the workplace. The first one was bad. A worker lost his marbles and killed another worker. I choose not to comment on this one because the guy obviously was just plain nuts.

The second story was about a worker in Oklahoma who killed his boss and injured his wife. This was fascinating because the killer worker was caught and was interviewed in jail. He matter-of-factly said that what he did was possible anywhere. He had been a good worker and was fired from his carpentry job. So he killed his boss. He related that he felt a level of frustration and betrayal that boiled over. The bosses wife whined that just because they had fired him he had no reason to kill her husband. Maybe.

Another story dealt with a family who was on the run from an escaped killer. The husband/manager had been killed over a work related dispute. The killer was placed in a mental hospital. And get this — they allowed him to walk outside unsupervised! So the killer is still on the loose and the family is on the run. They drive around from place to place looking over their shoulders and call the FBI for info. Unfortunately, what they don't know is that the FBI is far too busy infiltrating political groups to be bothered by one simple murder.

Another story was about a manager who had survived, unharmed, a worker rampage. The bossman had been turned into a complete zombie. A therapist, looking and

sounding like Mr. Rodgers, sat next to him and consoled him about not feeling guilty over surviving the shootathon.

But by far the best story was about the killing of bosses at an Alamo Rental Car business. The worker was a carwasher who was fired so he went to the office and offed two bosses. Management personnel and even surviving family members related that the management style of the big boss was through intimidation. One boss said he had been tongue-lashed in front of his employees by this boss. Anyway, after everyone was laid to rest, this tongue lashed boss was given a promotion. But after one day on the job he quit because he overheard his workers saying things like, "This is just the start, more of 'em are going to go down." I'm sorry but I burst into laughter at this point!

Finally, they ran a piece on postal assassins! This was like icing on the cake. The surviving people were so fucked up by the murders that one woman wore dark glasses inside her workplace. She said this was because it helped her to survive the day.

The show was meant to portray the anguish of the survivors. It did this effectively. But, TV is bossland to the max. They never seem to focus on the conditions that make murder possible. What are those conditions? Simple, corporations and bosses just don't get it. They think they can fire people without retribution.

Consider this scenario. You have a job, a family to support. You've been taught that hard work will win you a piece of the pie. One day you go into work and your job is gone. What do you do? Your hopes for the future are ruined. You are about to become a member of the dreaded under class. All this goes against everything you've been taught. You feel inferior, bills mount, tensions begin in the home. You snap and kill your boss.

Who created this situation? Corporate America and bosses have created this situation. They hate you and they hate me. They use us up and spit us out and have the audacity to believe we will accept the shit they throw in our faces.

KEFFO

It's a Bitter Pill to Swallow!

"My business is failing. The bank is about to foreclose on my home. My wife has left me and my daughter has run off to join a new age cult. I've got bleeding ulcers and a leaky heart valve. I'm ruined I tell you, ruined."

WHY?

"Because of those goddamned temporary workers, that's why!"

BOO HOO!

KEFFO

The Wonderful World of Temps

IT'S A JUNGLE OUT THERE!

COVER YOUR ASS!

CHRISTIAN ANGST

Unemployed? Why bother yourself with the stress that accompanies looking for a job when you can rely on your friendly neighborhood *Job Placement Service!*

Yes, highly-skilled career counselors are standing by right now, ready to lend you their wisdom and experience which will lead you to the new high-paying career of your dreams!

That's right, I can get you a job that pays ten thousand dollars a year!

Great! And you say your fee is only eleven thousand?

Looking to change your career entirely? It's no problem when you trust your future to caring, sensitive job placement personnel who are specially trained to discover talent inside of you that you didn't even know you had!

Good news...I can get you a job for minimum wage as a fry cook!

Wow! I *knew* that college diploma would come in handy some day!

Remember...When you rely on the services of your nearest Job Placement Service, you get the job while they do all the work!

Paid in Full

I had been unemployed for several months when I moved to Madison, Wisconsin. I had no complaints. After all, I had been able to balance the construction of my blue print for the future with a summer of near record beer consumption. But I had begun to feel the weight of all this empty time collapsing on me. I thought I needed to redefine my "work ethic." So, I went to a temp agency. The result was the secret perversion of all my politics and a classic example of the misuse and abuse of non-privileged labor in our flotsam centered system we call "America."

Sure, at first glance I was getting my needs and wants fulfilled. Most temp agencies have their workers on a sort of "on call" status. Basically, you can design your own work week by agreeing to an assortment of assignments. For those such as myself — the directionless, this can mean a way to get back into things at your own pace. The work itself is usually simple. Hell, it's less than simple. It's mundane. It's dumb. But that didn't mean I'd be missing out on any of the "fun."

My first assignment was a 3 day morning shift at the "World Dairy Expo" at $6 an hour. I was verifying data on the cows that farmers were entering into competition and acting as a "gate sentry." Confused? Let me give it to you in layman's terms; I spent a few minutes every morning corroborating with wealthy cattle ranchers, some from as far away as Japan and Australia, that their prize heifers had the correct teat sizes for their subdivisions to be contestants in the "Great Bovine Pageant." And "gate sentry?" Yep, you guessed it, an usher/security guard, responsible for seating people correctly. Admittedly, this doesn't do a lot for one's self esteem but, of course, it brought in some money. And, in retrospect, I'd do it again rather than act as a mislead prostitute for the big corporations out there.

And that's what happened. Slowly, I started to be aware that my assignments had a broader picture to them. When you're working as a temp you get into a comfortable rut

15

with the rudimentary functions of your 9 to 5. A sort of, "don't ask, don't tell, don't pursue," policy that you're lulled into. The non-temps generally treat you to a transparent, "Hello" at 8AM and "Goodbye" at 5PM. Your assigned manager tends to give you only the instructions necessary to complete your task (stuffing an envelope can be damn tricky!) while giving you the respect they'd give a vagabond.

Everyone who does temp work needs to look beyond their daily quota of phone calls and envelopes and ask: What does this company do? After my dairy stint, I had stuffed 15,000 envelopes for a local company denying domestic partnership rights to gays and lesbians. Not what any self-respecting fag likes to be unwittingly involved in! My supervisor even told me directly that, "Temps are thought of as purely disposable."

Still, the assignment that became a catalyst for me; the reason I thought about using my temp work to be a saboteur was from my work for a state-wide association of builders and contractors. Earlier in my life, I'd worked for years as a grassroots environmental organizer. Imagine my surprise when I realized one day that the phone calls I'd been making to re-establish members in this association were actually the first step in a campaign to initiate unknowing small businessmen into a national movement to rescind all current and already weak legislation on welfare policies and other "protected" biospheres!!!

Now I was pissed! I had been an ally to the radical rich and I wanted to do something, anything, to make personal amends to myself but didn't know what or how. In the end, the bastards gave me the tools themselves. I agreed to a one month assignment with a real estate/brokerage company. It was to be my longest stay with any one temp agency.

The company was a powerful, national company with strong stock ties to the nefarious labor hostile Greyhound corporation and had just been bought out by guess who — General Electric.

At first I had the warm and fuzzy task of vacating the desks of the employees caught in the middle of the buy-out and then stocking the storerooms. Some of the desks still had half-filled coffee cups on them! Some still had people in them, clearing out! Except for the other temps, there was a mood of frustration and disappointment. The whole scene sucked!

Then I was moved to the mail room and had the good fortune of being responsible for the placing and filing of incoming mail claims. Because of the chaos inherent in a staff changeover of that size, I had no supervision. I'm certain, there was no fear that any temp could do anything wrong to throw things out of kilter. They had placed me in a position to review incoming mortgage statements; documents that give financial backgrounds on people and their homes, and state whether they were paid in full, delinquent, or rejected and log them into their computer so they could be permanently filed. I could read the explanations for why they were late with their payments, whether it was due to a divorce, a job lay off or an out of control medical bill. I then insured that those who caused my ol' bleedin' heart to do just, were granted a break in their monthly mortgage payment. PAID IN FULL!

Of course, reading those bios and making decisions to categorize were not part of my job description. So, my hope is that some poor Joe out there had at least a month of unexpected freedom from the debt grip. All in all, I think some 10 to 15 people benefitted that day. And who knows? Maybe GE caught it or maybe they didn't. The point is, I had been misled by the temp agency into working for companies that don't give a damn for the little guy. But they had given me a monkey wrench that day.

And damn if I wasn't going to throw it!

JACK KEAR

Corporate Mailman!

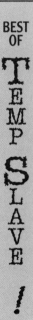

Another day pondering my declining financial situation. The phone rang. It was a temp agency calling to offer me a long term assignment as a mail and supply worker at a major insurance corporation. The code word "long term" is so appealing to the greenhorn, but in the temp industry it's nothing more than premature ejaculation. I took the job anyway because jobs like sex are sometimes hard to come by.

My job involved filling mail bins, going on mail runs, answering phones, doing specially collated mailings and filling supply orders. The squat ugly three story building I worked in employed 200 people and was the Eastern regional headquarters. The work was very customer service oriented and was the hub for operations on the East Coast.

I was met in the reception area by a nerdy-looking character who turned out to be my boss. A quick tour of the building ensued and then I was turned over to my trainer. My trainer was a crabby, frizzy-haired speed freak who was about to go on maternity leave. While it was her job to teach me all aspects of the job it was her intention to teach me the bare minimum. Anything more than that would be a threat to her job.

So for the next few weeks I listened to an endless, rambling description of my job. I smiled at the boss, played lapdog and quickly fell into the routine of regimented work for the corporados. This was usually my modus operandi at any job I worked at. It was important to make a good first impression because first impressions go a long way and the sooner you learned the job the sooner the boss man would leave you alone.

Mail and supply personnel are the plankton of corporate life. But you'd never know it talking with a mailer. Most mailers are perfectly content with their jobs because of fringe benefits and the freedom it entails. The job gives you plenty of opportunity to do your own thinking and the mail and supply department has less of a "business" atmosphere.

For example, my department of 4 people had access to office supplies, computers, a fax machine, a label making machine and a quality high speed copier. Best of all, was the opportunity to use company mailing machines for free postage. So almost immediately my best instincts took over and I began ripping the place off. Over the course of my employment I produced 3 zines on company supplies and equipment and paid no mailing costs.

The company I worked for was a renowned outfit in the insurance industry. It insured the richest people in America, mostly old wealth, movie stars and athletes. This is what they considered to be their market niche, leaving the Joe Schmo accounts to the lesser companies. Occasionally a policy would come across my desk and the obscenity that is capitalism became more apparent. Some of these folks owned objects of art done by the very best (mainstream) artists. Others owned rooms full of fur coats, jewelry and silverware. One couple I recall as having a list of possessions that took up close to 50 pages. Of course, the best thing to see was the policy of a movie star detailing his hideous collection of velvet clown art.

As a mailer, I had access to every person and area in the building. Often times I roamed around with no purpose in mind other than to witness how business was done and the reaction of people to their work. Processors, customer service people and underwriters toiled in small cubicles, pounding away on keyboards when they weren't

> PEOPLE . . . toiled in small cubicles, pounding away on keyboards when they weren't shoveling jelly doughnuts and low grade coffee down their gullets. . . .

shoveling jelly doughnuts and low grade coffee down their gullets. Long term insurance workers are easily identifiable by the immense width of their behinds. It is the march of the dead. One co-worker tagged these people with the name "desk mummies." It is an awful appellation but all so true. Some of the workers were complete ass kissers, others were in it just because it was a job. The vast majority were simply going to sell their souls until retirement day. Then they could wear loud clothing and travel on bus tours with other huge assed people.

> WORKERS are easily identifiable by the immense width of their behinds. It is the march of the dead. One co-worker tagged these people with the name "desk mummies." . . .

The building was run by a triad of smily-faced square looking white men in severe business suits. Five years earlier, this triad had been hired after participating in the decline of another insurance company. Once installed, they began cleaning house and continued to do so during my employment. If you weren't buddies with the top boys your existence was in doubt. The triad had a propensity for firing their managers while they were on vacation. A bland memo would go out saying, "He will be pursuing other interests." Then the clincher, "No one will take his place."

Like everywhere else in corporate America, downsizing was all the rage with the triad. There was no new hiring. If someone was fired or retired

they were not replaced. Or they hired temps like me without benefits to put the fear of god into the fulltimers. Why the workers allowed this to go on is amazing considering all the excess work fell in their laps with no increase in pay. The underworked/overpaid crowd had everyone in their place and reaped all the rewards.

But if you talked to a desk mummy about this inequity it was like you were speaking a forbidden language. Perhaps the long exposure to their VDT's had rotted their brains.

The culture of the workplace was another amazing thing to witness. The head of the company did all the correct humane things like squeeze money out of his employees for the United Way. This took the form of deductions from your paycheck, candy sales, hoagie sales, doughnut sales. The most humorous extortion gimmick was to charge people $1 to wear casual clothing on Fridays. Of course this meant business casual not boots, torn clothing or leather gear. Once while riding on an elevator with a Human Resource boss I asked if I could wear a dress and high heels on casual day. The boss glanced at me with his eyebrows raised and said, "No, because men don't wear dresses." I replied, "That's what you think." Whereupon the doors opened and she burst out of the elevator as if I had the plague. My mistake was to ask. I should have just done it.

Because the environment was so sterile and regimented, there were enormous opportunities to mess things up. Corporate offices are an excellent place for pranks and sabotage because even the slightest change is considered subversive. It doesn't even have to be outright destruction of equipment, rather messing with people's minds is even better. Phones, files, memos, paper supplies make corporate offices a prankster wonderland.

> **Perhaps the long exposure to their VDT's had rotted their brains.**

When visiting the records department I continually moved files from aisle to aisle so they couldn't be found. This became a big problem because the company was in the process of microfilming their files to do away with files altogether.

In my own department, if I came across mail I couldn't read or became overburdened with paperwork it was simply "disappeared." This is a common occurrence in all mailing operations since the abundance of paperwork makes it nearly impossible to track where everything is going. When challenged for an answer, some nameless person in the postal system could be blamed. It was a total win/win situation.

Another thing I did was mislabel envelopes by altering the names of agents. For example, the Cornwall Agency became the "Cornhole Agency" or the Brady Agency became the "Brady Bunch Agency." Sometimes instead of using a "&" between names I used a "$." But my favorite was the Artman Agency which became the "Fartman Agency." One friend mentioned to me that the use of "Fartman" would bring back terrible memories of his childhood being taunted by other kids. So that only made it better!

Answering the phone became my forte. A harried agent would call demanding supplies. Usually I took on different personas—the effeminate sounding Jonathan, or the deep voiced African American Benny. Sometimes I answered the phone in a deep voice and gave a woman's name. Most of the customers went along with it but other times I could tell they were thinking really hard about the person they were talking with. I suppose they were too embarrassed to say anything.

When I had some free time I gathered my co-workers around and did prank calls to other businesses. I looked in the want ads for the most God awful jobs imaginable and gave them a call. For example, a place called "Hot Dog Freddies" was looking for workers. In a monotone voice I described my credentials in the food industry and once hooked I began asking the person questions about working for "Hot Dog Freddies."

HF: Hot Dog Freddies, Mario speaking. May I take your order?

K: No, no I'm calling about the job advertised in the paper. Can you tell me something about it?

HF: Yes, the job pays $4.25 an hour and you'll be delivering hot dogs in a 3 mile area. There's also a 10% discount on food.

K: Do I have to wear a wiener hat or drive a wienie car?

HF: A WHAT.

K: You know, wear a wiener hat or drive a car with a big wiener on top of the car. You know like Oscar Mayer.

HF (*laughing*): No, nothing that extreme. But you do have to wear a uniform.

K: Does it have a wiener on it?

HF: No (*laughing*) look here's the address...

My co-workers had generally believed that I stepped off another planet but enjoyed seeing me get over since they could only think about doing the things I did. I was, after all, just a temp.

An overt stunt I pulled was to bring a puppet into work. The puppet was a nun in habit with boxing gloves on its hands and you could manipulate the arms to throw punches. I walked around the building on mail runs with the puppet on my right hand delivering mail to people. The reaction to this was hilarious. Some people thought I was just insane, others passed the word and a continual stream of desk mummies visited the mail room to see my puppet. So, for at least a few minutes they had left their work.

Rearranging the symbols of the corporation was another thing to do. The company set up a "Way to Go" program that recognized the very best ass-kissers. It was all mucky-muck bullshit created to perpetuate the myth that the company cared about its workers. Of course none of these workers ever got something real, like a raise in pay. A worker was nominated for a good business deed by another worker. The winner had their picture taken and a description of their good deed was included. It was then hung on a wall outside the cafeteria under the title "Wall of Fame." So once a photo and caption was hung I moved the text from one photo to another. No one could figure out who was making the switch.

Around Chirstmastime I found some flat plastic Christmas ornaments. One was an impression of a angelic looking child on her knees praying. So I made up a phony memo from the head of the company and mailed it along with the ornament to one of our more prestigious insurance agents. The memo read, "Like you, I pray that we have a profitable year with our insureds. But you never know, this could be the year when the whole ball of wax collapses on our heads. Let us all pray for each other so we can go out and make piles of money."

Other tales of pranks and sabotage filtered in from repairmen who fixed our equipment. One copier repairman related an experience he had at a law firm. He was called to repair a copier that had been sabotaged. Every time a copy was run, an image of a pen showed up on the copy. The frantic workers insisted that someone had jammed a pen into the copier and as a result the copier was out of use for 3 days. So the repairman went to the law firm and tore the machine apart wasting even more time with no luck. Finally, it came to him. Someone had pulled a timebomb prank. The prankster had made copies of a pen then inserted them into the middle of a pack of blank papers and resealed the packet. Eventually the packet was opened and used and pens began showing up on legal documents throwing the whole firm into a fit. When he informed the bosses, they hit the roof but by then no one could be blamed.

My co-workers could not do the things I did but they made up for it by being ace slackers with bad attitudes.

> The company set up a "Way to Go" program that recognized the very best ass-kissers.

Time theft, sick days, "lost" paperwork, stealing food from the bosses and other departments was the norm. Best of all, we read any mail with confidential markings on it. Outrageously funny stuff could be found. Often times we came across complaints from customers or read about the stupid shit people did that cause the company to pay out thousands of dollars. One customer burned down his house and the company paid out $100,000 but an agent noted that the customer wasn't reliable since he was arrested once for standing on his roof, firing a gun and screaming that America was being invaded by space aliens. Another time, two women were driving down a highway and began flirting with a truckdriver. They took their eyes off the road and caused a 3 car pile up sending everyone to the hospital. The flirting incident was duly noted in the report.

An even funnier thing was that the company by law was expected to send out cancellation notices by a certain date, otherwise the company would be forced to renew the policy. If not the company could be sued. One time an underwriter discovered that a customer was selling heating oil from huge tanks in the garage of his home. So not wanting to risk having to pay off a possible explosion, his policy was canceled and sent to the mailroom. Unfortunately, it got buried under paperwork and

$400 for a day's work seems like poverty ...to US

THE TEMPS ARE here... Take it easy.

© Don MacKeen '95

wasn't found until after the expiration date had passed. My nerdy boss nearly cried when he found it. He was forced to listen to a tongue lashing from his superiors.

Everything I did is justifiable when you consider what the insurance industry is. The industry is a humongous scam perpetuated on the public. In most states the insurance industry is not even regulated. This allows insurance executives to set rates according to their competition with no regard for the public good. A very select group of elderly white men maintain secrets like rats hoarding crumbs. In a sense, the insurance industry is a closed society of suit and tie thieves. Insurance companies bet that they can convince you that you are bound to fuck up so you better protect yourself. But, as insurance companies know, the vast majority of people don't fuck up and they are allowed to invest money from people who will never get a paycheck on their premiums. One finance and planning officer, giving a speech in my workplace, explained that the money collected from insured people covers labor costs and building rentals alone. What he failed to mention is that the rest of the money, billions of dollars in investments in real estate and stocks, is used to support a lavish lifestyle for the men at the top. On the other hand, while insurance companies don't like paying out to policyholders, a fuck up, whether it be a fire, natural disaster, theft or insurance fraud is an opportunity for the insurance company to raise

premiums on the hapless consumers who never have any trouble.

So unless an insurance company is run by complete idiots, the industry can never lose. The deck is stacked against the consumer. This is all apparent when you understand that the industry sets the rates and a gullible public buys into it as witnessed by the billions of dollars in profit each year by the suit and tie monsters.

Another factor for troublesome employee behavior is the nature of temporary work. In a historical context, the temp industry is an extension of the job shark operations that existed in the early part of the century. The job sharks advertised jobs to the unemployed. When the unemployed arrived for the jobs they were surprised to find that they were competing with thousands of workers for a limited amount of jobs. The worker who was able to get a job soon found out that they were nothing but slaves since they could easily be replaced. Only a militant response to these unfair tactics brought an end to the practices.

While the more extreme instances fell by the wayside, the job sharks modified their tactics with the establishment of corporate and worker friendly temp agencies. Much like the situation in the early part of this century, in 1990's America, the corporate elite have made it known they don't give a shit about workers. Temp agencies and corporations work hand in hand, making sure that pay is kept low and benefits are non-existent.

Considering the horrible employment situation in America, this is a wise move on their part since many workers are fearful of losing what little they have. With little or no prospects for job creation, the temp industry is quickly becoming the job of the future. So with this in mind, there is no reason whatsoever for a temporary worker to feel any kind of loyalty to their job and company. In fact, with nothing to lose or gain, it becomes all the more imperative for a temp worker to strike back in any way possible.

Anyway, my actions did not cause the insurance industry to grind to a halt but it sure made my work day bearable.

KEFFO

Dishwasher Temp!

After a few leads that led nowhere, the job opening at the hospital (in Dayton, Ohio) seemed ideal. The catch: I'd be working through a temp agency (leeches that need to be eradicated from the earth) and I'd have to take a drug test. I never thought I'd ever consider pissing in a cup for a dishwashing job, but since I knew I wouldn't be at the job for long, since I did need some cash, and since it seemed so strange it was almost appealing, I took the test. No one at the drug screening place seemed sympathetic to my comments—"All this for a dishwashing job?!?" Just as the government has planned, this nation has been desensitized toward any concerns of a urine test. It's accepted. Well, my appetite for poppy seeds didn't flunk the test for me — so I was hired.

The hospital's basement dishroom was a sprawling operation. There were anywhere between 3 and 8 dishwashers cranking out cleanliness on any given shift. Among these fellow dishwashers were guys in their early twenties, women in their fifties, laid-off employees from the auto industry, a woman who was a publisher before her current 6-year stint on this crew, a guy who owned a doughnut shop for 30 years until he got sick of making pay-offs to the health inspectors, police inspectors, fire inspectors, etc...and one guy who had been in the dishroom for 23 years, man, I couldn't get over this fact. And yet he was the happiest guy there. It has been 11 years since I stayed at a job for more than 9 months straight — I like quitting too much to break any endurance records. Anyway, all these folks were cool to work with. One day I was waiting for the bus when a car slowly passed by and someone waved to me. I was stunned. I thought I knew her — but this wasn't a work situation—so it was difficult to recognize this co-worker. It's as if you turn off your TV and then there's a knock at the door and it's Fonzie waiting to come in.

It took awhile to play into the abundant free eats. Dishroom eating was "grounds for dismissal." But I longed for all the untouched food on the trays brought down from the patient's rooms. It wasn't any such fear of being fired that kept me from munching away, it was my fear of hospitals. I've never been laid-up in a hospital and the only experience I've had in visiting hospitals was when I was 10 years old. My friend Jimmy shared a hospital room with a kid who refused to take his medicine. So they put it in his food. At least that's what the nurse told us—probably doing

26

it to keep us from pilfering his food (free food was the main reason lots of neighborhood kids visited Jimmy). Anyhow —looking at the food on the trays and imagining the drugs they contained kept me away from any nibbling. Eventually I was clued in to where the eatable eats were stashed (over by the pot washer's area). Since we were all trying to be discreet about our munching, there was a roomful of dishers walking around with their mouths stuffed, cheeks puffed out, slowly and slyly chowin' away.

My favorite activity here, besides dropping the glassware that crystallized real cool before shattering, was simply sorting the silverware. It was the one position you could walk away from, hide out, and not be missed. Some of the guys were notorious for disappearing for an hour or two.

When it came time to quit, I called the temp agency and told them I was on drugs, tripping out, and felt it would be dishonest for me to continue working since they wanted someone who was clean. They told me, "It's OK—what you do on your own time is your own business." Yeah, right, so then why was the test required in the first place? After that I simply stopped answering their calls for me to come into work.

DISHWASHER PETE

27

Temporary Insanity!

As you sit at the abandoned desk of a complete stranger, you move from being annoyed with the unfamiliar to becoming obsessed with pure chaos. You experience a deep-seated and overwhelming urge to reorganize. And so you begin stacking. Stacking is an easily accomplished task and one that can be done while you answer the phone and struggle to remember who you're working for and where you are. Although forgetting who you are is a definite occupational hazard, it is not something that actually matters.

You begin slowly, perhaps unconsciously, by restacking the rectangular objects — notebooks, message pads, staple boxes, pen boxes, envelopes, miscellaneous labels, computer and company policy manuals, and the ever present sticky-memopads. All things flat and rectangular are grouped together in one drawer and aligned with precise, if uncaring, angularity. This stacking is similar in nature to the universal human pastime of stacking pocket change into small, conical pyramids according to the size but not the value of the coins. Stacking according to actual utilitarian nature is virtually meaningless. The only variation encountered between stacking coins and stacking office supplies occurs when a truly plentiful array of stick-pad colors is available. In this case, the stacking is always done in accordance with the laws of diffracted light as exhibited by a rainbow.

After completing the various stacking tasks you are free to rearrange the office hardware. While moving the phone and computer system around the desk is not the same as organizing in any formal sense, it gives you the opportunity to familiarize yourself with the peripherals at your disposal. Many happy hours can be spent faxing your friends or exploring the local BBS with your employer none the wiser. Should anyone question your desire to move the computer, you simply tell them that you are concerned with potential VDT damage. Because of every employer's wish to avoid a possible lawsuit, you find that they usually leave you alone.

Next you determine the outside boundaries of your domain. You go through the inevitable assortment of unlabeled keys and try to discover which drawers and file cabinets they unlock. This task usually takes 3 to 4 hours and provides you with reason to

scope around the entire office floor. You discover the supply room at some point during this task — a good end in and of itself.

After you have located and explored all drawers at your disposal, you begin to impose order within these new territories. Simply alphabetizing is not enough. You do a ground-up renovation and regroup things according to company, project and year. You go through all the files, writing down the pre-existing categories. Starting from the existing categories, creating larger, unifying groups as well as smaller, more precise sub-divisions. You create computerized label templates. Creating, or even using, a computer gener-

ated label template impresses your coworkers, demonstrates your command of technology, and saves you the untold hassle of actually walking to the office's single, archaic typewriter.

There are obvious and not so obvious advantages to this approach to filing. One of the most obvious is that you are always able to produce a particular document on request. While filing is tedious, it is infinitely more tedious to work within the parameters of the pre-existing "system." The existing state of things is always chaos. You never create an illogical system, and you always create a written guide to your system. Failure to fulfill either of these criteria is contrary to the sublime and unspoken ethic implicit in ordering.

The not-so-obvious results of reorganizing the hard-copy files is that everyone trusts your talents as you begin to reorganize the computer files. People tend to be nervous when you play with the computer mostly because they themselves have little knowledge as to what lurks within the machine. However, once you have spent valuable time organizing the objective hard-copy filing system, people will think you are a rare, earnest, and ultimately trustworthy worker. Once others trust your organizational savvy they will ignore your exploration of the ethereal computer world which is the single most important component within your temporary world.

While reorganizing computer files has some of the same obvious effects as reorganizing the hard-copy files, the not-so obvious benefit of reorganizing the computer files lies in the discovery of hidden applications and programs. While icons associated with the pre-packaged computer games that are bundled with Windows are usually removed, invariably the games themselves still exits. Organizing the computer files allows you to locate these games, and helps you determine where in the system to hide your own personal games. You always bring your own disk(s) of games to a long-term job. The secret is knowing where to hide the games in the system, how to play them silently, and whether or not hitting Escape will simply hide the screen or also stop the game's progress. Some early games of Tetris continue to run in the background, which completely ruins your high-score average.

> **You cannot escape its imperfection. The unsightly sin against perfection is in your face! You want it to go away. It does not BELONG! It must be eradicated, wiped out, obliterated, hidden. You refuse to acknowledge its existence.**

While there are many beneficial and positive results of organizing the world in which you temp, you must never lose sight of the golden rule of the organizational process. Organization is first and foremost and must always remain a completely emotionless act. You do not organize things because the things want to be organized. You do not arrange things because you want them to be arranged. You do not organize because order matters. Organization is not pleasurable, it simply occurs. Organized things are not a joy, organized things merely display an order. Emotionless action and emotionless reaction is the solitary buffer between your sanity and your soul.

If you forget this principle, you begin to revel in the act and the outcome of the organizational process.

You have organized the computer, the files, the keys, the labels, the rolodex, the papers, the pens, the tablets and the miscellaneous. You have created order from chaos. A place has been defined and set aside for everything, and everything is in its place. You have sorted the unsortable. You have distinguished the indistinguishable. You have named the unnamed and labeled the anonymous. You have created place and space and placed all things. As you glorify your actions and marvel in the clean perfection of order, you experience a desire to continue ordering. You no longer act to act, you act to order; you act because you want order. You feel imperfection lurking amid your perfect creation. The large paper clips with the micro groves in their wires mingling amongst the large paper clips without micro groves. There are two keys WITHOUT names — keys unimaginable, unknowledgeable files. There is one, single solitary, unique interoffice envelope from the London office which is NOT STAN-DARD. Its excessive length and sinuous narrowness, its grotesque foreignness mar the perfect coherency of your envelope stack. The disorder is unsettling. The uniqueness is evil. Places must be found so these things can be placed. Their imperfection must not exist within your order.

You hide the unique offenders in the dark recesses of the farthest, bottom most, unused file drawer. You close the drawer, shut out the knowledge of this imperfection, return to your ordered desk and bask in ignorant contentedness amongst perfect order. You smile as you survey all that you have wrought. Order has flown forth from you and perfection mirrors your very being. Your eyes caress the smooth, blank desktop with perfectly aligned objects. The labels scream out names that you alone have bestowed. You know every thing and every place and every function. You sit in the center of absolute control. Absolute power is yours. You have sorted and filed and classified. You have named the unnamed and have given meaning to all things. You can destroy all of this and bring back the abysmal chaos whence your order emerged.

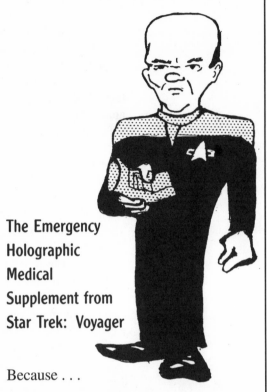

TEMP OF THE MONTH!

The Emergency Holographic Medical Supplement from Star Trek: Voyager

Because . . .

1 He was only meant to be a back-up but has become indispensable

2 No one knows what to call him.

3 He has no rank.

4 He knows infinitely more than anyone gives him credit for.

5 No one ever tells him anything

PAUL T. OLSON

31

Your eyes glide over to the computer terminal. You despise the random pattern of stars and have done away with the frivolity of screen savers. The screen of your computer terminal is clear and black. As you gaze into the face of dark perfection, an image begins to emerge. Slowly, the clear, infinite depth of the blackness begins to crystallize, revealing a seeming symmetry of ovals and curves. You blink at the apparition in the screen. You direct motion in the image. You blink again. The image becomes more clear — two arches, two ovals, a triangle, an outline. You focus more intently on the image. Your eye for perfection notes that the right arch is not quite the same as the left arch. There is a minor variation in the curve. Your desire to root out the unique spurs you on. You look closer. The right oval is different from the left oval! Or is the right oval a more obtuse version of the left? The imperfect symmetry staring in your face is a blight on the once perfect screen. Wishing to block out this imperfection, you blink again. The image blinks back. You cannot escape its imperfection. The unsightly sin against perfection is in your face! You want it to go away. It does not BELONG! It must be eradicated, wiped out, obliterated, hidden. You refuse to acknowledge its existence. As you realign the desk calendar and the phone and your desire to order is once more fulfilled, your power validated, and you shut out the haunting image of imperfection.

HEIDI POLLOCK

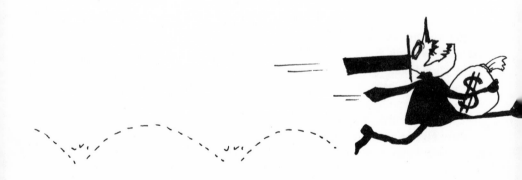

My Dream Temp Job!

Considering everything I've said about the temp industry and considering everything I've done while working as a temp, I wasn't exactly thrilled when I had to get a temp job again. But you gotta do what you gotta do.

One day I walked into the offices of the local agency and told them to reactivate my file. I nervously glanced around, expecting a net to fall on me, buzzers to go off and thugs come rushing out of a room to beat me within an inch of my life. Nothing of the sort happened. Instead, the cheerful industry worker gave me a look over and said she would call me within days.

Later that day I was offered a one day job at a huge retail warehouse setting up shelves for a major paint company. I roared with laughter when a few days later I received a letter detailing what was expected of me at this job. Besides the usual ass-kiss stuff the letter ended by saying, "THANK YOU for accepting this important assignment! We appreciate your willingness to take part in this project. The next time you walk through the paint department of this store you will realize how nice it looks and that your help made it this way!"

By the tone of the letter it looked like they were going to bust my balls the whole day long. So I wasn't too encouraged about the whole situation.

The day of my assignment it rained. Outside of the building the lot was a quagmire of mud. The macadam for the building had not yet been paved. So you were forced to walk over mounds of mud and pallets laid down to make walking easier.

I reported to the receptionist and waited for my one day boss to arrive. Four other people showed up and we wound up lounging around the reception area.

The regular workers began arriving too. At starting time, a huge group of them gathered around their bosses and listened to their orders for the day. Suddenly, one of the bosses began yelling "Ok what's No. 1!" The workers screamed back their answer, "CUSTOMER SERVICE."

MARSHMALLOW BOY GETS A JOB

COOL! A JOB!

FLAME THROWER FACTORY →

HELP WANTED

IT'S A DANGEROUS JOB, BUT I NEED THE MONEY...

WHOOSH

DANGER! TESTING AREA →

...AND MY COWORKERS SURE ARE FRIENDLY.

SNIF

MMM

HM.

S. CONROY 96

NEXT WEEK: MARSHMALLOW BOY LOOSES HIS HEAD ON THE JOB

My jaw dropped and one of the other temps shook his head and laughed. I couldn't believe this kind of feel good crap went on. The workers were willingly allowing themselves to be turned into puppy dogs. For what, I really don't know.

Anyway, an hour passed and the boss still wasn't there. We looked quizzically at each other. Finally, I decided to give the agency a call. They told me that the boss was stuck in traffic somewhere and that I should call back in an hour. So in the meantime, I wound up talking with the other temps, who turned out to be pretty cool people.

Another hour passed so I called again. This time they told me that we should wait one more hour (until 11AM) and if the boss didn't arrive by then, leave and mark down that we worked to noon. This was too good to be true! This was a dream! The kind of temp job I've always been looking for!

So the five of us sat back, looked at mags or stretched out on shelves. The eager beaver receptionist eyed us and told us to keep our muddy feet off the shelves. When she turned around I dug my heels into the shelves. Time began ticking away. We all agreed to leave at exactly 11AM and not come back that day if we were called. The prospect of 4 hours of pay for doing nothing became intoxicating.

Finally, 11AM arrived and we bolted out of the door, laughing our heads off and telling each other how much fun it is to work with each other. This was definitely my kind of temp job.

KEFFO

10 Tenets of Temping

1 Work as slowly as possible. This establishes a norm, allowing you to set the pace, not them.

2 Come in a little late, leave a little early, take long (or multiple) lunches.

3 Don't work at all when possible, but always look busy. Develop a repertoire of tricks for looking "busy" while actually doing nothing.

4 Pilfer as much as possible — look for new ways to create your own business. Suggestions: office supplies, photocopying, faxing.

5 Find out if you can make long distance calls and faxes on the company account, then milk it for all its worth.

6 If your bosses are assholes, begin a carefully planned sabotage program, taking extreme care to cover yourself. Leave "time-bombs" if possible, that will erupt after you leave the assignment.

TEMP OF THE MONTH!

Michael Stagger works as a temp guinea pig for a drug testing laboratory. Michael likes chemicals, injections and loves screaming his head off in public places.

WAY TO GO MICHAEL!

I WANNA PLAY VEGAS!!

HEY, GET ME MY WALKING CANE PRONTO!

WAAAAAAAAAAAAAA

HAPPY TEMP INC.

"Old rock stars NEVER die. They JUST ANNOY EVERYONE."

7 Deny knowledge of any job skills other than the basics; advanced abilities lead to more difficult assignments at no extra pay.

8 Use the workplace to do all personal business: call friends, write letters, read books and magazines, etc.

9 Play mind games with yourself to stay sane (e.g., "I'm a spy who has infiltrated 'their' operation, and 'they' must not find me out.") This will protect your mental health in mind deadening assignments. Remember: You are better than them.

10 Play dumb. It works.

TEMP X

Temp X is obviously an intelligent worker. He covers the main themes of getting by on a temp job — sabotage, theft, slacking off, playing dumb and using your brainpower to outwit the bosses. Remember, the only power you have at a temp job is the power of your own imagination.
Thank you TEMP X!

I Get A Real Temp Job

The temp agency was seriously messing with my head. They continually sent me to job interviews where I had no chance in hell of getting a job. I didn't want to have to dress up in a monkey suit for $6 an hour. I couldn't afford to look nice. So I asked the agency to send me to jobs that were more laid back. I really shot myself in the foot this time.

The very next day I was sent to a major department store in a mall to work for a company that was redesigning the whole store. In effect they had been contracted out to give the store a new customer friendly retail look.

I was to work from 6AM to 4:30PM Monday through Thursday. A rotten half hour lunch and two 15 minute breaks for $6 an hour. The first day I was called late so I arrived at 10AM. I stood around and watched people put up warped shelves. One worker said, "Oh man it's only 10. I'm not going to make it." I knew I was in for some heavy shit.

Sidewalk Bubblegum ©1995 Clay Butler

Finally, I was pulled aside and told to unload a truck. I worked with another guy who informed me that he had been a temp on this job for 10 months and had never missed a day of work. I looked at him as if he was psychotic. But, as a result of his loyalty the design company had offered him a job, traveling around the Northeast setting up stores for $12 an hour. So it turned out he was the favorite of the boss. But it also turned out that this guy, despite being loyal, was also a con artist. He had perfected the art of ass kissing but always found time to screw off when the boss wasn't looking. We worked the rest of the day together and it really wasn't too bad.

The next day, though, the alarm clock went off at 5:30AM and excuses were running through my mind. But I went anyway. This day was a total slack day, I set up shelves and carted building materials to a dumpster but most of the time I walked around looking busy but doing nothing. The fun part was getting to know some of my co-workers. One guy was just hilarious. He had the uncanny knack of looking at customers and blurting out the names of media stars who looked like them. "Mary Lou Retton!" and then a short and stocky woman walked by. "Elvis Costello!" and then a thin older man with an ungodly pompadour and thick black glasses came strolling in. I began laughing so hard that tears came to my eyes.

He then told me about his experiences in the Marines. He had been in the Marines for 10 years and had been in Beirut during the bombings, seeing many of his friends killed. He had taken shrapnel in his back and legs and the Marines booted him out on a medical discharge. He had been a drill instructor at Paris Island and had made recruits stand in line near a mosquito pond. Black flies buzzed in their ears, eyes and up their noses. This caused the recruits to make funny looking facial gestures since they were not allowed to swat the flies with their hands since they were at attention. He and the other instructors stood behind the recruits and asked them if they were cold or asked if they were having seizures. While I dislike the military and the mindless things involved in the military, I couldn't help but laugh visualizing the scenario he described. After all, funny is funny.

The customers were another sight to behold. The main clientele was older people. The kind of people who had store loyalty. Suffice it to say, to be as kind as I can, these old codgers were rude, evil and nasty. They frequently stood in the way and when you said, "Excuse me" they looked at you as if they would stab you. One old farty woman started mouthing off at another worker because he was carrying something on a hand truck. The worker was at a safe distance, but the woman must have had vision problems, or hemorrhoid problems or whatever. She started screeching that the worker was not paying attention to where he was driving. We witnessed this, shook our heads and laughed.

At one point I worked with two other people in an enclosure. One side a narrow window was built into the wall and it looked out onto the women's clothing section. Right next to the window, outside, was a woman mannequin so the three of us took turns striking poses in the window as shoppers strolled by. We picked up tools and acted like we were hacking at each other with drills, handsaws and knives. One of the others mentioned that he would bring in a noose, wrap it around his neck and pose in the window. Again I was getting a kick out being on the job.

But of course I got pissed off as usual. For one thing, since the store was going through a major redesign a lot of goodies were being thrown into a dumpster. I could not believe my eyes. I actually saw the store and the company I worked for throw out stuff like chain saws, chairs, picture frames, filing cabinets, and loads of construction material. I eyed this stuff like a treasure. I asked around and found out that you first had to ask to take it and pay a reduced price. This totally infuriated me because if you didn't pay the price they would throw it out anyway. I totally ignored this rule and rescued clothing, filing cabinets and whatever else I could smuggle out of the dumpster. Everyone else did too. One day I looked into a dumpster and

> . . . so the three of us took turns striking poses in the window as shoppers strolled by. We picked up tools and acted like we were hacking at each other with drills, handsaws and knives. One of the others mentioned that he would bring in a noose, wrap it around his . . .

one of the carpenters was removing a thermostat from a heating unit. He declared, "These fuckers are stupid, this part alone saves me $30 if my unit goes bad!"

Everything I saw only reinforced my previously held opinion that America is a wasteful country.

The job alternated between being extremely hard one day and easy the next. Strange things happened. One morning, about 5 minutes to opening, a squirrel got into the store. Groups of workers tried to corner the rascal but it got away each and every time. I laughed, and watched grown men and women running up and down aisles searching for the squirrel. Eventually it was cornered in a room and then set free.

Temps came and went. The job really sucked. But a few temps lingered on, including me. My co-workers were complete ass-kissers. One had installed himself as the "foreman" of the temps. The other two were Puerto Ricans.

If I ever hear someone say that all Puerto Ricans are lazy then I'll say you're full of shit. In fact, the Puerto Ricans I have worked with are hard workers. They are not lazy, however like all ass kissers, they are dumb workers. Maybe it's machismo or maybe they think they have to prove themselves, but, this was a temp job!

There was a language barrier between the three of us, but I made my sentiments plain and clear by saying, "If you work hard, how much do you get paid?" They replied, "$6 an hour." Then I said, "And how much do you get paid if you work slow?" They looked at me and mumbled, "$6 and hour." Eventually, they understood that I was not going to speed up my work no matter how much they tried to bust my ass. In any kind of construction work, the new guy always gets the shit jobs and this is how you "prove" yourself to the other workers. Some can hack it and others can't. I could hack it but I wasn't about to break my back doing it.

Out of all the workers on the job site, the laborers were the only non-union workers. The electricians, carpenters and painters were all union. This interested me so I wrangled a job as a helper for the carpenters.

The union people were unbelievable. They were slow workers, time thieves and thus the smartest workers of the whole lot of us. They dumpster dived like there was no tomorrow. One guy even brought a trailer to work to haul stuff away, right under the noses of the bosses. These guys were cool about work but often times not so cool when it came to certain things.

One day, I hung dry wall with a 64-year-old carpenter. At first glance, I thought he was an old fart. But as it turned out he was a passionate supporter of unions and working people. I learned this by asking him a single question about the site. Mainly, why was his union so chicken shit that they allowed non-union laborers like me on their site?

He paused and then let loose a blast. "The American people are the most

CHRISTIAN ANGST

fucking ignorant people in the world! All they do is cry about unions but it was the fucking unions who got them all the benefits they enjoy. Even a fucking 8 hour day for most of 'em. But, to answer your question, the reason we are so chicken shit is because we are weak. When Reagan fired the Air Traffic Controllers the whole country should have gone into revolt. But what'd we do? We wanked ourselves. I even went to convention where Reagan spoke and my business agent told me to respect the Prez. I told him to fuck off and I walked out when Reagan took the stage. I've been in this racket for almost 45 years and at one time we wouldn't even work if there were non-union people on the site. Today we take any old thing that comes our way and we can't do a thing about it!"

This old guy, nearing retirement had more common sense then all the others I met on the job. When the business agent for the union visited the site the old guy tore into him each and every time calling him a "sell out cocksucker" to his face. The agent had recently negotiated a job that paid the union workers only 60% of their standard rate. I never laughed so hard in my life!

The other guys were humorous in their own right. The painters stumbled around all day long and did nothing. The carpenters acted as if they were god's gift to the world. A lot of them consider themselves the elite of the American workforce. I have no doubt that they wear their tool belts to bed.

Being a carpenter is their whole reason for being. It cracked me up because I could have given a shit. They were high wage clowns with belted armor.

Everything you may have thought about construction workers is the truth. They are sexist, racist and arrogant. One guy I worked with continually whistled at every woman who walked by. This embarrassed me to no end since I wasn't about to get blamed for harassment. So one day I called him on it. I asked him if he had any sisters. He said he had 3 sisters. I then asked him how he would feel if they walked in and I started making lewd comments. He looked at me as if I was out of my mind. He just couldn't make the connection. But it did shut him up at least when he was working with me.

To be truthful, though, the nature of the job and the people you work with makes it impossible to be respectful of anyone or anything. There is absolutely no stopping these guys and after awhile I gave up. You have to consider the whole picture. Most of these people are surrounded by men all day. Stinking, dust covered men, decked out in tools and work boots. The place you work in is completely ugly. At times it takes on a homoerotic aspect. A few of the carpenters referred to each other as "honey" or "dear" and told me they like to be patted on the ass. This was done jokingly, of course, because these people were straight as arrows. But I think part of their behavior stems from not being around women, except for their wives. So when they see an attractive woman they go absolutely bananas. In fact, their main form of recreation was to scope women. If a particularly attractive woman walked through the site, the word was passed, tools dropped and the whole crew ran to a good vantage point. I love women too but the difference is I didn't stand in the open making myself obvious, with my eyes popping out of my head, my tongue hanging out, making grunting noises. I wasn't so obvious.

Racism is a given. The whole crew was lily white. The one temp who was the "foreman" palled around with one of the Puerto Rican temps. When he wasn't with him, smiling at his face, he bitched to me about mixed couples, "niggers" and "pork chops." I wondered if his good buddy knew about the words he used. The whole situation overall was somewhat like the military. They realized that in the trenches color didn't matter, but inside their hearts they were scared of different looking and acting people.

But even having said all this, I'd be lying if I said I disliked them. In fact, despite all their flaws, I liked them a lot. The reason I liked them was simple. They were aggressive, direct, and didn't play mind games with you. They were as genuine as anyone I have met in my life. They were always up for a good argument on almost any topic and the hilarious thing was that one minute they sounded like a left wing nut on a single political issue and the next minute you thought you were talking to a Nazi. It never failed to interest me or amaze me.

Dealing with the bosses was their forte. Tradesmen know their job. They seldom need supervision. As one carpenter explained it, the best kind of boss is a boss who shows up, tells everyone what jobs need to be done, and then goes away. Unfortunately, our boss was looking to make a name for himself so he continually looked over your shoulder whenever possible. But, because he lived 3 hours away he left work early, so as soon as his car moved 1 foot from his parking space the whole crew began packing up their gear and running to their cars. Sometimes, especially on the last day of the week, we left work one or two hours ahead of time.

Finally, this pissed him off and he called a meeting. He explained that the job was over budget and we could no longer rip him off on break time or leave work early. A short silence ensued, whereupon one painter blurted out, "Are you leaving early this week?" We all began laughing. He was

> When the business agent for the union visited the site the old guy tore into him . . . calling him a "sell out cocksucker" to his face. . . . I never laughed so hard in my life!

defeated and the usual routine was maintained.

The budget issue brought the biggest snickers. One guy explained that every single contractor used the same song and dance. They always pleaded poverty but not one of them ever went out of business.

The one day the bossman was in his serious mode he approached me and a few of the other workers. He looked at me and said, "One of our crew is leaving for another job, you know the score, you know what needs to be done here, so we will be relying on you to keep things together." My mouth hung open I couldn't say anything. As soon as he left the carpenters began laughing and saying things like, "Yeah, we know you and you know the score!" It was funny, because there was no way in hell I was going to be the baby sitter for the other workers. I considered myself "standing labor," I stood around while other people labored. Bosses are really fucking stupid sometimes!

Despite the more humorous aspects, the job sucked. It was back breaking and every single day brought an ache or pain to different parts of my body, blisters on my hands and feet and a general feeling of tiredness. If you had an easy day you were damn sure that the next day would be a killer. Because there was demolition work, I was the person who had to cart away heavy stones and bricks to the dumpsters, plus, whatever else was being thrown out. My back was a mess.

The only fun thing I can remember was the day I was told to move a display unit through the store so it could be assembled. The unit was packed in a box 15 feet long, 2 feet wide and 5 feet across. When I went to load the box I was surprised to learn that someone had drawn a picture of a hugh fat man the length and width of the box. Plus, the artists had drawn a 3 foot long penis on the man, outlined in red marker, to boot. I burst into laughter again. The temp foreman brought the bigwig store managers over to take a look since I would be taking the box through the store and customers would see it. They milled around, staring and rubbing their faces with their hands for a few minutes. Finally I broke the silence by saying, "Hey, if it really bothers you I can draw shorts on the fat guy." They began laughing and told me to take it through the store.

So I put the box on a cart and ferried it through the store. It was so huge that it looked like a perverse billboard. I loved it since I could see the reaction of people when I walked by. One elderly Vietnamese woman took a look and scrunched up her face as if she was sucking a lemon. Another woman and her husband started pointing and laughing. The store employees looked and had huge smiles on their faces. When I arrived at my destination I pulled the cover off the box and stood the drawing right side up so everyone could see it. I then did a theatrical bow and people applauded.

Alas, all good things must come to an end. The bossman, oily as ever, tried to butter me up. He took me to lunch for pizza and afterwards he approached me and the temp foreman. He mentioned that a laborer was needed for the third shift. The foreman indicated that I would do the job but I would need more money. The boss rolled his eyes and said, "More money? Well, what the hell does he want, I bought him pizza!" This made me completely furious. For the rest of the day I cursed at him or gave him the finger behind his back while everyone was looking. I decided then and there that I wasn't going to work on the site anymore.

Our shift ended on a Thursday. The third shift started on a Sunday night. I waited until Friday, 5 minutes before the agency closed, to inform them that I wasn't going to put up with their low paid back breaking shit anymore. Either they gave me a raise or gave me a new assignment. The agency worker was incredulous. She had no idea that the work conditions were so bad. Or maybe she did and was playing stupid for my benefit. I asked her why so many other people had quit working at the site. I also asked her why the agency was sending people to a construction site and not telling them that they needed to wear boots and gloves, the standard gear for any site. (In fact the fuckers didn't bother to tell people they would be doing construction. Some temps arrived wearing shorts and sneakers! So much for safety!) She offered her apologies and assured me that the agency was not in the business of sending temps to dangerous work sites. It was all bullshit because temp agencies don't give a crap about the places they send people. What they are not used to are their people calling them up and telling them how rotten their jobs are.

So by informing the agency of my plans late, they could not assign another temp in time to take the job. Everyone got screwed — the carpenters had no one to cart away their materials so they would be bitching their heads off at the bossman. The bossman would have to endure their complaints and worry whether or not the job would get down on time. The temp foreman would have no one to work with, making his job even harder. The agency would be placed in the position of not being able to fill the slot. As for me, sure I wouldn't make any money that week, but on Monday morning I slept in for the first time in a month with a smile on my face.

The thing I regret about the job is the fact that I did not get the assignment earlier in the year when 30-50 temps were on the site. Without a doubt I would have been organizing sick outs, walk outs or sheer defiance for better pay and conditions. In the end, when temps understand their shared interests then the game is over for the industry.

Two days after quitting, I received another call from the agency. They offered me another job.

A few weeks later I ran into one of the carpenters I worked with. He told me that when Monday morning arrived, no laborers had shown up to work. The carpenters began harassing the boss man by asking them where I was. The boss glumly looked at his feet and muttered, "He quit because I didn't pay him enough money." Whereupon one of the carpenters laughed and said, "Of course he quit, you dumb ass, you wouldn't give him a measly extra dollar an hour to work. You deserve what you got and by the way, we need help so you better find somebody else pronto or else we ain't doing shit today."

The agency did find some bodies and they were put to work scrubbing grunge off the tiles in a bathroom. Within a week, they too had all quit.

KEFFO

African-American Temps

Temporary companies are a tool for increasing the power of the bosses over the rest of us.

Much like off-shore money laundering operations or shell corporations used by the rich to avoid taxes, temporary companies are a legal shenanigan which allow the bosses to get around laws for which many workers, fought and died.

For instance, when I'm out on assignment, I work for some company that pays me through a temp agency. This slight monetary detour changes my relationship with the company for which I actually produce things. I produce just like any other worker whether it be cars or memos. The only difference is that the company farms out its payroll and human resource department in the form of a temp agency. By doing this, they are able to fundamentally change the legal relationship with me, their employee. I no longer have the right to organize a union. They can fire or refuse to hire me for any reasons including political,

BEST OF

T
E
M
P
S
L
A
V
E
!

"YOU TAKE MY LIFE WHEN YOU DO TAKE THE MEANS WHEREBY I LIVE" —SHAKESPEARE

racial or gender prejudice. And furthermore, because industrial temps are usually desperate to become permanent workers, they are expected to behave in the most obedient fashion.

The temp agencies are crucial in filtering out any expectations for regular raises, health benefits or even basic human respect in the workplace. Temps are paid less than regular workers, even though, we do the most degrading or repetitive jobs. Even if you include the temp agency's cut, it costs companies less to use temps because they don't have to pay for benefits like health care or unemployment insurance.

The bosses profit and power on the shop floor is increased enormously by using a temp agency.

It should then be no surprise that temp agencies are used for controlling and depriving the rights of the most troublesome (for the bosses) and radical elements within the U.S. industrial working class: African-Americans. Several studies have shown that African-American workers are staunchly more pro-union than any other race or ethnic group in the U.S. Employers know this, and as a result, blacks often suffer from racist hiring practices in the permanent economy especially in cases where companies are trying to avoid unionization. Consequently, a disproportionate amount of African-Americans are forced into the low-skill temp economy. Industrial temps, approximately 1/3 of all temp workers, are disproportionally African-American.

Larger demographic and investment trends in urban areas have contributed to the growth of African-Americans in the industrial temp economy. Industrial production has moved to the suburbs during the last twenty years. This has left the African-American working class stranded (because of poverty, lack of transportation or racial discrimination in housing) in the cities. Some temp agencies use this desperate situation to force large parts of the Black working class into the role of permanent temporary workers.

Dolphin Temps, for instance, specializes in shipping African-American and other urban-trapped workers to the suburbs. Dolphin has a fleet of vans that deliver workers to the point of production three shifts a day.

Dolphin establishes contracts with factories, guaranteeing that they will produce so many bodies for every shift. It is possible to go to the Dolphin offices in the morning and be shipped out that afternoon on a second shift

> It should then be no surprise that temp agencies are used for controlling and depriving the rights of the most troublesome (for the bosses) and radical elements within the U.S. industrial working class: African-Americans.

job. Workers report that they often board a van without even knowing which plant they are being sent to.

An important aspect of this system is low-skill production. The production process has been so de-skilled in many industries that almost anybody can competently perform many factory jobs after a few minutes of training. Workers are always replaceable and interchangeable. Consequently, it is companies that perform low-skill production which use temp agencies the most.

Industrial temps are paid $6 or $7 per hour, about $200 per week if you can work a full 40 hours. However, the temp agency charges the workers $4 per day for a ride to and from work in the vans. They also dock pay for not picking up checks at an established time. Industrial temps are often sent home early if a job is finished or too many people are sent by the temp agency. This results, of course, in loss of wages. There is little compensation; workers are usually given at least two hours pay. Nothing is guaranteed.

I worked for a couple of months as a temp in a plastics factory. At this place, it was very clear that African-Americans would never be hired into permanent positions. There was only one permanent black worker on my shift. Generally, if you work for three months the company is allowed to hire you away from the temp agency without being charged a finders fee by the agency. But one black worker had been at this factory for 6 months and had still not been hired as a permanent. Meanwhile, several other temps had been hired ahead of her. The message was clear to the other African-Americans: this is not the place for you.

This racial caste system is evident time and again. I worked at another factory which assembled framed commemorative prints of sports stars. The entire wage work force was temporary! Ninety percent of the workers were black, all of the office personnel were white. The half dozen supervisors were both black and white.

Tony, a co-worker from the plastics plant, was a 24-year-old African-American who lived with his girlfriend and two kids. We came to the factory on the same day, and for my two months there, I gave him a ride to work every day. He raised my consciousness concerning the racial fault lines running through the temp industry.

Tony was eventually told not to return to the plastics factory because he asked a supervisor not to treat him so rudely. This simple request for decency was beyond the toleration of a supervisor, typical in her demand for absolute obedience from the workforce. That is, after all, what they are paying the temp company for.

A further complication is the racism of the white working class. Many white workers in suburban factories actually live in small towns as much as an hour drive outside the suburbs. Their experience with and understanding of the problems of the city are minimal. This largely permanent white workforce works daily with under-skilled, under-trained, under-paid, low-commitment, black workers. While permanent workers are right to feel threatened by temporary workers, the racial lines created by this system simply feed into all of the television-generated racial stereotypes.

For instance, Tony had been working as a temp at a unionized shop. But even there, the animosity and racist distrust was thick. When I asked him why he quit his job at the union shop he just said, "I felt like somebody was

Work! Work!

always watching me, always looking over my shoulder. You just can't work like that for very long. I just couldn't take it anymore."

These are just a couple of examples of the new levels of obedience demanded of the industrial temp and it is directly related to our powerlessness on the shop floor and in the law. This powerlessness leaves us open to a level of coercion not experienced by permanent workers.

Temp workers must find ways to fight back. We must seek forms of collective action — whether it be unionization or some other form of political action in order to demand basic workplace rights.

SAM SMUCKER

T
E
M
P
S
L
A
V
E
!

The Secret Life of Temps

They come and go quietly, huddling behind their PCs and Xerox machines, no desk to call their own, gripping styrofoam coffee cups while sneaking glances at the advancing hands of the clock on the wall. Temps are silent slaves of the corporate ogre, the indentured servants of the modern plantation. The question is, who owns the plantation? The temporary agencies or their clients? The agencies, like the slave owners of old, earn their profit through a couple of quick phone calls, while the clients cut costs by saving on the cost of health care and benefits for their one-day-at-a-time work force.

CONGRATULATIONS! You've worked twelve hours a day, every single day for forty years. Your dedication and committment has enabled our corporations and temp agencies to realize record profits. During that time, you came to work every day never knowing if that day would be your last day. It's very difficult not knowing what the future holds and soldiering on in the face of adversity. But, rest assured, your contributions have not gone unnoticed. As part of your retirement plan, we've decided to let you take a peek at the future. Look at the clock, in exactly 7 seconds you will have a massive stroke that will kill you. Thanks for your time and nice knowing you.

This message was sponsored by your friends corporate America. They also furnished

My personal experience as a temp has given me first hand experience at how dehumanizing it is to be part of a workforce of millions that must do the bidding of their masters with no hope of a future or advancement within their work environment. The temp is little more than another corporate expense, like the office houseplant maintained by a paid contractor — when one dies, throw it out and get another. People working as office temporaries report feeling invisible in the office: they are often not introduced to other employees, not given the respect of "full timers," and are usually sitting in someone else's workspace, which creates a sensation in someone else's workspace, which creates a sensation of living in someone else's apartment — nothing is familiar, and nothing is yours. The temp is a ghost, a shadow of a "real" employee.

The psychology behind the temp phenomenon is important in understanding the dynamics between him/her and the company. Usually, an office temp is called when a regular employee is absent or, worse, when a company is in a crisis and needs an extra body to help with the avalanche of work. Either way, the company is resentful from the beginning because they are paying two people for one job, spending precious company money to deal with the crisis. So the unfortunate temp is walking into a situation where the company already resents his/her presence! Resentment breeds contempt, which leads to the generally shabby treatment given most employees.

The employer, therefore, does not see the temp as a real person with a life outside the office — the temp is merely an expense, something that has been purchased and must be used to justify the expense. In my "real" life, I'm a musician, and I'm always amused at how my bosses react when they find that I do something besides interim employment; there is a genuine reaction of surprise, a sudden twist in reality, a look that says "how can this be?" I am supposed to be a temp and nothing but a temp. Do they think I was born a temp, like being part of a caste that is destined to a sub-strata of the workforce? Do they think that anyone would want to temp given the choice?

Sadly, many attitudes toward temps are similar to those toward homeless people: the common knowledge is that they must have done something bad to end up like that, and that therefore they deserve to be there; they look the other way when they see us coming, not knowing what to say; they toss us some work to do and shuffle away, angry at having to have us there in the first place or embarrassed at having forgotten our name (again). We temps really are the itinerant workers of the office, wandering from desk to desk, living off the scraps of others.

Perhaps another way to see the reality of temping is to look at a typical day on the job.

A DAY IN THE LIFE

The following is an account of a typical day on the job by Henry B.

"I arrive five minutes early for a 9-5 assignment only to find that the job is actually 8:30 to 5, so I'm already late (the agency's fault; one of many miscommunications that take place regularly). I'm rushed into a cubicle by a supervisor after a hasty introduction to her boss — they plop me down in front of one of those old green screen monitors connected to a 1973 era mainframe computer and begin an elaborate log on procedure without bothering to show me what they're doing. (Of course, I have not been shown where to find the men's room, the lunch room or vending machines, how to make outgoing phone calls, what time my breaks and lunch are, etc....)

"Now I'm logged into this stone-age computer and the supervisor begins flooding me with insanely complicated instructions for retrieving and modifying information in their system. At no time has anyone told me (a) what this company does, (b) what this job is for, (c) why I've been hired. I'm then given a stack of papers and left on my own with the instruction "Just come and get me if you have any trouble." I look around the room I'm in is painted white — white walls, ceilings, desktops — and hundreds of florescent lights cover the ceiling. Images from Orwell's *1984* come to mind as I begin the mundane task that will occupy 40 hours of my life per week for the next seven days.

"Luckily, the other employees turn out to be friendly, but they are so deadened by their work that any attempt at conversation drift off into mumbles. Plus, they know I'm "The Temp," so conversations with me, are in a way, forbidden. No one wants to be seen talking with the temp because it would be a loss of status in the office political culture.

"I find out where the men's room is by exploration, and begin scoping out office supplies and the copier room for future reference. As the day goes on I am amazed that the full time employees actually work in this place every day and seem actually somewhat content. Work like this has a numbing, hypnotic effect on human beings; and then I suddenly remember that I'll only be here a week and am momentarily glad to be a temp."

It is true that there are times when temping is a good thing — mainly when you're stuck in a job from hell. Knowing that the last day on the assignment isn't far away can be an inspiration enough to keep slugging it out through what would normally be unbearably tedious work. And that very common feeling underscores how bad it really is for many temps.

BUT, there's another side to this dismal picture: The Agencies! Next issue I'll talk about the temp companies and all their dirty little secrets.

MALCOLM RIVIERA

Thank You for Calling Sega

There are 12-year-old boys who would suck your dick to have the temp assignment I just completed. For the last three months, I went behind the scenes of what most kids consider the coolest company in the world. I worked for Sega of America's Consumer Services Department. I spent eight hours a day answering the phone and getting berated by angry parents whose children's videogames weren't working.

The department was staffed by about a hundred phone reps, most of whom were temps. Our primary function was to talk people through the installation of Sega's home videogame system, the Genesis.

If you consider the demographic you're dealing with, you'll understand that this job was a prescription for misery: videogamers tend to be losers. They have no friends. They sit in their dark little rooms with the curtains closed, playing *Mortal Kombat* while the rest of us are out there having lives. From this demographic, there is a special sub-class: those who are too stupid to connect a Genesis to a TV. These are the ones I dealt with.

The stupidity of our callers was usually a function of age. I often found myself talking to 10-year-old pieces of shit who could barely tie their shoelaces, but somehow had mastered the brainpower to dial our 800 number. Kids are passionate about the industry. They would sometimes ask me, "How do you get a job at Sega?" I worked for the company that created *Sonic the Hedgehog* and *Altered Beast*. In their eyes, I was the luckiest guy in the world. I was part of the inner circle and they wanted to talk with me for an hour.

Our callers' passion for videogames had a dark side. It was damned easy for them to become irate. Adolescent boys would call just to harass us: "Why do you guys make such crappy games, man? I think Nintendo really kicked your ass with *Donkey Kong Country*. You guys don't have

anything to compare with that game! I've got over a thousand dollars invested in Sega products, and all you give us is crap! I guess Sega just doesn't care about their customers. I think Sega fuckin' sucks man." Blah, blah, blah. Like I care.

I felt like saying, "Listen, you little punk, let me get you alone in a jail cell for two minutes and I'll beat you until blood comes out of your ears." But, I couldn't say that because our calls were randomly monitored.

Once a week, my supervisor would listen in on two of my calls and then grade my performance. He used a scorecard of Standards and Expectations, which was a list of things we were supposed to say in every call. "Thank you for calling Sega" was supposed to be the first thing a customer heard when we answered the phone, and the last thing they heard before we hung up.

The worst thing about the job was that it was an endless grind. Day after day, you had to listen to one irate parent after another, all with the same complaint.

"We sent away for a free game promotion over 3 months ago and it still hasn't arrived! I've got a very impatient 5-year-old who asks me where his game is everyday. I've called you people twice already and both times you've assured me it's been shipped and I'd like to know where it is ...." Blah, blah, blah. I listened to that complaint hundreds of times.

If the customers weren't getting what they wanted, they would fly off the handle. The stupider people would threaten legal action, "The store told me I could get a free game if I bought Sega and now you're telling me I bought the wrong system? This is bullshit and if you don't do something to make me happy, I'm going to the State Attorney General and the Better Business Bureau." Now there's somebody with a keen understanding of our legal system! One bitch threatened to take her story to "some big radio station." Yeah, right, I'm sure the news director will devote at least an hour of air time to your complaint.

In almost every case, Sega had done nothing wrong. It was grueling to take this abuse and I dealt with it by using my favorite stress reliever: Sabotage and theft! Here's a brief overview of my activities:

MASTURBATING AT WORK: The computer kept track of every minute you were logged on the phone system. You were expected to be logged on for a minimum of 7 hours and 15 minutes a day. This made it especially thrilling to run into the bathroom and furiously pump my erection, knowing my time was limited. Having beat off in a wide variety of work environments, I've mastered the art of the quick jerk. I could usually have a satisfying fantasy and reach orgasm within 2 or 3 minutes.

DRINKING ON THE JOB: One day, during lunch, I decided to get bottles of OJ and load them up with vodka. I gave one to the guy I shared my cubicle with and we were pleasantly buzzed for the rest of the afternoon. On that day, we had a "stress buster," which means we got to log off the phones early and have a pot-luck party. I still had plenty of vodka, so I turned a few of my coworker's beverages into cocktails.

ANTAGONIZING CUSTOMERS: In spite of the possibility that the call was being monitored, sometimes I just had to make these people unhappy: "You want to talk with a manager? Well, I hate to say it, but my manager's not gonna tell you anything different from what I'm telling you. There's just no way Sega's going to do what you're asking .... "

FREE SUBSCRIPTIONS: If a customer was irate, we could set them up with a free subscription to *Sega Visions*, the company's magazine. This sub normally costs $14.95. Needless to say, every friend I have now has this magazine coming to their house.

ADDING CUSTOMERS TO MY SHIT LIST: The Shit List is something I've been compiling for several years. Having worked in the service industry all my life, I've been abused by all sorts of customers. I've often had access to my customer's phone numbers, addresses and credit card numbers. If somebody was nasty to me, I would record said info with the intention of tormenting them until they die.

The easiest way of doing this is to fill out those little postage paid magazine subscription cards and check the box marked "Bill me later." The customer then gets magazines they didn't order and bills they weren't expecting. For this reason, the raunchier porno magazines don't have "Bill me later" cards, but *Playboy* and *Penthouse* do.

Some of those subscription cards even give you the option of sending gift subs to other people. This service makes it possible to have one asshole customer get billed for mags being sent to some other asshole he's never even met.

Of course, sub cards are for amateurs. The next level is credit card fraud. You call a mail order catalog and pose as your customer, using his credit card to have crap sent to his house. I do feel sorry for the phone rep from the catalog who will eventually have to deal with someone screaming and

SILLY CAPITALIST
TRIX ARE FOR EVERYONE!

CAPITALIST PIG...
THE OTHER WHITE MEAT!

GOT MILK?

JUST DO IT.

Sidewalk Bubblegum ©1996 Clay Butler

yelling because merchandise the customer never ordered is arriving at his house and being charged to his credit card.

Mail order catalogs are happy to send gift orders, so, as with the sub cards, you can have one schmuck sending products to some other shit-

head he's never met. If you're lucky enough to know the name of your customer's wife, you can have him send her expensive flowers or other presents. Most catalog companies will include a gift card that says, "From your adoring husband" or whatever. Imagine the predicament of your asshole customer when he comes home from work to find his wife creaming all over herself, thanking him for the beautiful jewelry. He can't very well say, "I didn't send you that!"

Unfortunately, catalogs dealing in porn usually send out disclaimer letters telling your victim that he's about to receive smut in the mail. The recipient must send a little card back to the company stating he does, in fact, wish to receive smut. This makes it difficult to have Butt Pirates Abroad and The Unbearable Rightness of Peeing unexpectedly appear in someone's mailbox.

A word of caution: credit card fraud is serious business. If you get caught, the authorities will bury your ass in a hole so deep, you'll never get out.

Another great thing about my Shit List is that I can make it look like my customers are harassing people. A friend of mine had this boss, who we'll call "Ann." Ann was a bitch, and she was making my friend's life unbearable. I had this customer, who we'll call "Jim." Jim made my life unpleasant for a few minutes. I wrote Ann a letter on Jim's behalf. The letter started out by saying, "Hello, I got your name off the Internet. I understand you're interested in YOUNG LOVE and raunchy piss play. You sound like one hot little number!"

I had Jim go on to describe the things he'd like to do to Ann. Jim happened to live in a town close by, so I made it clear that he traveled to Ann's city often, and that he and his wife would love to get involved in "a variety of hot and horny scenes" with her. I made sure Jim's spelling and grammar were erratic and haphazard in order to convey a sense of dangerous insanity.

MISUSE OF COMPANY MAIL: We were provided with all the envelopes we could use, because customers were always requesting instruction manuals, promo materials and game-play hints. Nobody thought anything of it if I sent out 20 large envelopes a day. Naturally, I felt the need to steal things from the office and mail them to my friends. All of my friends. Every day.

Sega knew we were a bunch of temp scum. They made sure there was hardly anything in the office we could steal, so I had to get creative. I would send confidential documents, memos on how to dispose of confidential documents, memos on awful, hidden flaws that surfaced in our products and so forth.

In my desperation to steal something, anything, I stole packets of tea from the employee kitchen. Sega provided us with all the tea bags we could use, in various flavors. One friend received 20 packs of tea every day for a month straight. He was able to host wonderful tea parties as a result.

Sega also provided packets of instant soup, so I sent a lot of those out as well. Toward the end of my assignment, it occurred to me to snoop through the emergency medical kit. It was a cornucopia of over-the-counter pain killers and PMS medications, as well as lewd rubber gloves! Needless to say, I stuffed countless envelopes with these things.

I wanted to find new and interesting items to put in the daily care packages from Sega but there just wasn't much for me to pilfer. I started bringing garbage from home and mailing it; ten year old copies of People, dirty cartoons, unknown pills, used Kleenex, I didn't care. I just had to send shit!

So there it is. Life at Sega. You'll notice I spent a lot of time complaining about my customers, and not much time talking about Sega's faults. As temp jobs go, Sega wasn't all bad: I got eight bucks an hour, forty hours a week. I could park my ass in my cubicle all day without seeing the boss, so shaving and showering were optional. We could play all the latest games in the lunch room, and our immediate supervisors were cool.

So, why was I dishonest and subversive? Well, I've been sabotaging employers for so long, it's become second nature. It's in my blood. I couldn't stop if I wanted to.

BRENDAN P. BARTHOLOMEW

BEST
OF

TEMP SLAVE!

Goodbye to All That

In the distant future, work will no longer be necessary or possible because society will have realized that work is wasteful or because there will not be any jobs to do. Thus, when the historians sit down to write their massive tomes about Work, they will title a section of the book, "The Worst Jobs Ever" and under the title will be a photo of me. Or if a shit-job museum opens it will be named after me. I'll be famous because the great work god has parted his cheeks and taken a long dump. And the shit has hit me each and every time.

My farewell to the great state of Pennsylvania was another in a long line of indignities. Let me tell you about my last temp job in PA.

Quitting my laboring job saved my back but it didn't save my soul. That was left for my temp agency to suck out of my body. They assigned me what they termed a "good" job as a records clerk at a major chemical company.

I thought it would be a cakewalk but the minute I drove onto the grounds, a security officer leapt in front of my care and furiously started taking notes. I knew I was in for some more shit. I was given a pass and a parking permit and then instructed to go to the main lobby. A worker from records met me and the two of us then descended into the bowels of the facility.

Before I give you the gory details I need to mention the company. It is perhaps one of America's largest pigdog polluters. Until recently, it was run by a right-wing republican who practically owned the local newspaper and politicians. He continually warned that "his" company would leave if taxes went up. Scared shitless, the locals kissed his rear end. It was a cozy relationship.

The facility was monstrous and was the world headquarters. At least 5,000 people worked there and it was so large that shuttle buses were needed to carry people to different parts of the facility. It had a cafeteria that served food all hours of the day and it even had a money machine so people could access

money. There was an all-weather track so the yuppie management types could exercise. By corporate standards it was first class. By my standards it was obscene and hell on earth.

Anyway, I was shown to my desk. My co-worker, a woman in her mid-twenties, explained the job. My job was to sit at a desk all day long and sort through boxes of files looking for any material relating to hazardous waste dumping. Everything else was to be thrown out. A huge recycling cart was deposited in front of my desk and I began sorting through the mess.

At first, I barely found anything. The job became more like recycling — I pulled the clips and rubber bands and metal fasteners off files and dumped the files in the bin.

The job was completely insane! This is what I supposed to do forever. My co-worker smiled when she explained that this was it. After a few days, my head was in a cloud. I was burned out. I decided to take a closer look at the files instead of just looking for magic code words. I began to learn how big business is done.

The company designed power plants, sub-stations, nuke plants, oil refineries and any other grubby kind of job they could get their hands on. Their specialty was the chemical process though. They did not actually build the

> . . . **if a shit-job museum opens it will be named after me.**

plant; they designed and bid on contacts. Once they got a job they contracted the work out to other companies. Say the design cost $5 million. The company would then try to get the work done for 2 million and collect a tidy profit. They were the engineering "brains" behind the whole effort. Other people did the actual construction.

The bidding process on the work usually involved 4 to 5 other contractors. Of course, the company awarded the contract to the lowest bidder. This was smart and also stupid as I was to find out reading further into the files.

Projects began and ended right there in the paperwork before me. Buying a low bid seems the thing to do but in some cases leads to all kinds of trouble. The company didn't give a shit if the workforce was union or slave labor, just so the work got done. Three things always seemed to happen in the end: 1) The contractor was a bullshitter and couldn't do quality work. 2) The company designed the plant in a shoddy way making it excruciating for the contractor. 3) Lawyers on both sides sent nasty letters back and forth arguing about technicalities.

So, having said all this, does it make you feel better that these are people who construct nuke plants?

I'll be famous because the great work god has parted his cheeks and taken a long dump.

Reading about smaller projects was also a lot of fun. Internal memos stating that a certain contractor was "delusional and paranoid" or memos stating that equipment ordered for a plant was so messed up that to correct it would mean paying out the same amount of money as the original bid were par for the course.

But the over riding theme in these mini-dramas was the fact that business is dog eat dog. One time I came across a purchasing file on a company in Minnesota that did good work. No matter, the eager-beaver purchaser at my company said, "They do quality work, but like all long time suppliers they will get sloppy so it's time to wake them up. Let's give a percentage of their contract to another up-and-coming company just to keep them honest." Months later, the main supplier had lowered their prices to keep their contract and the purchaser gleefully patted himself on the back for his good deed. I just wondered if he knew that the loss of business to the company would mean some poor working slob would be out of a job for lack of work. Alas, there are no such concerns in the world of big business.

Other times, I read of companies who skewered their competition with damaging info, just to keep the company down. Then the purchaser would write an authoritative letter to the put upon company insinuating that their company put out a bad product. The funny thing is, no amount of back stabbing or dirt guaranteed a contract.

I tried to picture these boring rodent like businessmen at work. No, I tried to picture myself kicking their asses, each and every one of them.

Every once in awhile, I found some corny company PR manuals that various corporations put out. One company, a transformer insulation business in Ohio put out this thick glossy book, all about insulating transformers. At the end of the book the genius of the owner took over. For at least 10 pages, he pontificated on his conversion to a conservative Christian sect. I was amazed, astounded at what I was reading in a transformer manual! I laughed. I really laughed.

But no amount of drama, corny manuals or back-stabbing could make the job bearable. It was completely boring. So god awful boring that I felt like I was asleep with my eyes open. I began to dread another day at the drudge mill.

I began to not pay attention to the files. When the boss went to her office, I simply threw the files in the bin without looking at them. I didn't give a shit if I found anything. I had hoped to smuggle info out of the department because it was obvious that the Feds

And the shit has hit me each and every time.

were cracking down on them for their environmental criminality. Instead of pirating info, I decided to just throw it away since the lawyers would have a fun time explaining to the Feds why they didn't have the correct paperwork. What could they do to me even if I was nabbed. After all, I wasn't the polluter.

The office I worked in was dead silent, except for the sound of fax machines and the occasional announcements over the intercom. My boss was an older woman who walked around talking to herself. Which in some respects was better than my co-workers who frequently mumbled like lunatics.

The door to our office was a dual door, the kind where you can close the bottom half and open the top half. Despite the top part being open, the boss woman insisted that the bottom half be locked at all times. I wondered if this was done to ward off attacks from crazed dwarfs. My boss also had a hard on for safety. I sat at my desk for a half an hour listening to her babble about the scourge of paper cuts. She demanded that anytime I was cut, I was to wash, disinfect and wash again. She told me the horror story of someone who had gotten blood poisoning from the dreaded paper cut. After working a construction job the thought of a paper cut being fatal was almost too much to comprehend. I sat there like a bobbing dog head toy in the back of a car, nodding and saying, "Uh huh, Uh huh....." She just wasn't my boss, she was my mother.

I think my presence on the job was curious. Everyone had nice clothing and the men dressed in newly pressed white shirts. I wore wrinkled green, red and blue shirts that blasted your eyes when you looked at me. At the end of the day, people took side exits to get to their cars. I continually walked through the main lobby where all the big wigs hung out kissing each others asses. It was like going to the zoo. They were the animals and I was the visitor.

The really bad thing about the job was that I couldn't steal anything of value or use their copying machines. When you can't do that at a temp job you know it's a bad temp job. Plus, the job reminded me of being punished. It was like having to write, "I will not talk in class" a thousand times.

My co-workers were a load of fun too. Both of them were back stabbing busy bodies. Every so often they would look over my shoulder to see that I was doing the job properly. Once they caught me throwing files away without looking. I went ballistic on them and yelled that it was highly unlikely that a company that sold paper products would be carting haz waste. But, then again, maybe they knew more about the pigdog company than I did. I mean anything was possible with this rotten company.

Just to stir the pot, I told them both that I was quitting at the end of the second week. They looked at me as if I was pulling off a great betrayal. I secretly think they loved it since my copping out would make them look all the better.

My final day arrived and I carefully arranged a humorous time bomb prank as a farewell. The boxes I pulled files from were stacked on a pallet. I unloaded some of the boxes and then slipped subversive leaflets into the files so that the next person who took my job would find them. I then put the boxes on the bottom of pallet and restacked them. Thus, I would be long gone before the leaflets would be discovered. Some were straight forward and the others were completely obscene. I figured it would give the next worker a belly laugh or even better, a shit fit. Maybe the temp would even run to the boss and show her!

My shift ended and the boss woman asked me about scheduling. I cut her short and told her I wasn't coming back because the job was too boring. She looked like a ton of bricks had fallen on her head. Instead of harassing me, though, she started bad mouthing the agency saying that they had been "futzing" her around for over a year. I joined in, calling the agency losers, hopeless and beyond help. I walked out of the building with a huge smile on my face.

Early Monday morning the temp agency called. The rep said she heard that I had quit. Then she tried to lecture me, saying I should have contacted her

N OLD IRISH SAYING

Iay those that love us,
    love us--
nd those that don't,
    may God turn their hearts.
nd if God can't turn their hearts,
    may God turn their ankles.
 we'll know them,
    by their limp.

Thousands of bosses!
Thousands of cripples!

first. I gave her my best "I don't give a shit attitude." It was humorous. They were bummed because I chose to quit on them without informing them of my plans. If I had, they probably would have fired me. They got screwed and they knew it. The rep went on to say that now she was in hot water with the company. Apparently, my boss woman had reamed her out and the rep didn't know how she was going to fill the position.

I paused and said, "Oh, that's too bad. By the way, you can deactivate my file because I no longer want to work for the agency anymore. You have continually sent me to low paying, horrible jobs and I don't want to do it anymore."

There was a long pause on the other end of the line and then an even longer sigh of resignation. I tried to muffle my laughter by putting my hand over the phone. I then said goodbye and hung up before she could say anything.

Congratulations are in order. Yes, I was rude as hell, but deservedly so. Agencies and businesses, like pimps and paying customers, use temps like prostitutes. Only I was able to give it right back and they never saw it coming.

I look around and what do I see? I see buildings, roads, cars and all the other aspects of life as we know it. Who built everything? Working people did. Who maintains this life? Working people do. We do all the work and we get very little pay back for our efforts. Our bosses live in luxury, issuing orders and living off the fat of the land that we working people created. It's time to put the fuckers in their place. We don't need them but they certainly need us. Withdraw your labor, by far it is the most effective thing you can ever do.

Temps can learn a few lessons from their jobs. First, never tell the agency when you are quitting. Second, never tell the bosses when you are quitting until the very last moment. Third, always be direct with your agency reps and bosses when the time comes. They are not used to stand up people and when faced with one it gives them a migraine headache. Fourth, always leave a little reminder of how much you hated your job for the next person.

See you at my next temp job.

KEFFO

My Last Temp Job?

I was a Kelly Girl. It sounds pretty strange to say it now, but I really was a Kelly Girl. It happened during my last semester of college. I was hoping to gain some professional experience and earn some money as well. Everyone in the know told me to go with Kelly. They said Kelly would take care of me and look after my best interests.

I made an appointment and went in to find out about my future with Kelly. The ultra friendly Kelly Bosses encouraged me to take numerous software, typing and grammar tests to find out what sort of wonderful assignments I'd be eligible for. Of course I scored well on these tests. I watched exciting videos detailing my responsibilities and rights as a Kelly Girl. I was ready for any challenge Kelly could sling my way.

A call finally came one blustery January afternoon. It was a Kelly Boss: "Mr. Rigler, it says on your application that you once worked in a copy store...?"

"That's correct," I replied in my most business-like tone.

"And it says that you are good at binding, collating, and that sort of thing...?"

"Of course," I chirped, my bosom full. "I am quite familiar with those procedures."

"Well, that's just great because we have a job lined up for you," she said, almost as excited as I was. "Tomorrow, show up at the —— firm at 8AM. Mr. —— will explain your assignment when you get there.

The next day just couldn't come fast enough. I sprung weightlessly from my futon and rushed to the shower. I imagined what my coworkers would be like. Would they like me? Would they laugh at my jokes? Would they go for an after work Fresca with me? My head swimmed with possibilities. I quickly shaved, slathered on some deodorant and got dressed.

The bus arrived right on time as usual. I bounded aboard to get out of the steady drizzle and found a seat next to a kindly

Work! Work!

old man with a flatulence problem. Even his rank, intestinal stinkiness couldn't put a damper on my glowing mood.

Mr. —— met me in the front office of what turned out to be a large building. The room was adorned with the taxidermied heads of dead animals. I followed him through the building to a cavernous room, where he handed me a piece of paper and pen. "You need to sign this," he said, matter of factly.

When I started to read the paper, he seemed confused, perhaps a little annoyed, but the Kelly videos had admonished me to read carefully any document I was supposed to sign. The piece of paper said that as a trained temp, contract-labor employee, I would receive a wage that was technically lower than minimum wage. The document went on to claim that should the company be unhappy with the quality of my work at the end of my one week period, they could legally refuse to pay me one red cent.

"C'mon, just sign it," Mr. —— persisted, "It's just for our records. We can't pay you unless you sign it."

I just knew that Kelly wouldn't send me on any sort of questionable assignment, so I put my doubts behind me and signed the paper. He folded the paper and gestured to a row of tables at which sat 3 or 4 employees. "Take a seat over there next to that stack of paper."

I quickly seated myself and looked up at him, beaming. Mr. —— picked up an odd-shaped piece of paper from the stack, bent it in a few places, then glued it with a strange tool. He placed the completed object, a folder, to my right. "Got it?" he asked, somewhat sarcastically.

"You mean, this is what I'll be doing for this assignment? No binding, collating, or that kind of thing?" I asked, incredulous.

"This is it. Time to get started. Lunch is at 12:30." He walked off.

I decided to take stock of my surroundings. The room was actually a warehouse, no, a factory. A paper-products factory, where all sorts of things are made from paper. There was loud machinery and strange smells that made me a little queasy. It was then I noticed the music — loud country and western tunes were played over the PA, occasionally interrupted by announcements from the nasal voiced receptionist I had seen up front.

Shaken, I thought I would try and do a few folders. I folded one up and was about to put it on top of the one Mr. —— had done, when I heard someone say, "Nope, that ain't right." I looked over and saw a middle-aged

The next day just couldn't come fast enough. . . . The bus arrived . . . I bounded aboard to get out of the steady drizzle and found a seat next to a kindly old man with a flatulence problem. Even his rank, intestinal stinkiness couldn't put a damper on my glowing mood.

polyester-clad woman. She seemed to enjoy the work and took great pride in it. There was a tall stack of completed folders in front of her. "You better do it right if ya wanna stay 'round her f'long," she offered. I pretended not to hear and continued. The Kelly videos had said to never engage in office gossip.

Five or six folders later, my head began to ache. I felt so confused. Why would Kelly send me on such a strange assignment? Was it some kind of test to find out how loyal

I was? I decided that must be it and tried to carry on. The insightful woman to my left began to sing along to the country music. I winced.

Fifteen folders later, I began to feel somewhat nauseous. The chemical smell burned my nasal passages and my hands were throbbing and sticky with glue. My skin looked horribly pale in the artificial lighting of the factory. My doubts resurfaced. I thought of the battery of high-end tests I had performed so well on and the promises of good jobs, great jobs even, made by the all-knowing Kelly Bosses. I simply was not the right person for this particular assignment. Why, the day before, I had turned in a research assignment about middle-high German love poetry. I was intelligent, well-versed in political thought, and a darn good speller to boot. What had gone wrong? What had I done to deserve this? How had I raised Kelly's ire? I had to find out.

When I stood up and backed away from the table, no one seemed to notice. Mr. —— was several feet away. I walked directly to him. He looked up, surprised, and began to say something but I cut him off. "There's been a mistake. This isn't the right assignment for me. I'm sorry but I just can't do this." He said something sternly, but I only nodded absently and turned away from him. As I walked

> "Hello? Hello? I'm Here! I'm ready to work — honest!"

toward the front office, my pace quickened.

Soon I was out in the rain. Luckily the Kelly office was only a few blocks away. I trotted toward it, still believing I was the victim of a simple mistake, a mistake that would be worked out by the time I arrived at the House of Kelly.

I walked in the Kelly office breathless. The Kelly Boss who had arranged my assignment saw me and motioned me over, hanging up the phone. She was angry. "What happened? Mr. —— said you just walked off the job! What was so wrong that you had to put us all in such a bad position?"

I slowly explained the situation at the paper factory, the smells, the sounds, the "pay contract," the nature of the job itself, everything. When I was finished, I felt relieved.

My Kelly Boss wasn't buying it. "There was nothing wrong with that assignment. We picked it for you because we wanted to see how versatile you were. I don't think we'll be able to give you anything better if you can't make do with what we give you."

Suddenly, my confusion was replaced with anger! Who was this woman? Did Kelly approve of what she was doing? I didn't think so. "Look, if those are the types of assignments you're going to send me on, you can just forget it. Find some other fool." With that I turned and left. Everyone in the Kelly office, including some new Kelly inductees, stared at me as I hurried out.

It took a few weeks before I realized that Kelly would never vindicate me. Perhaps Kelly no longer had control of the business, like some figurehead monarch. I gave up on Kelly and thought about getting a job with the (gasp) IRS. My life had reached a new low. My friends couldn't console me, no matter how many times they put on nuns' habits and played Twister to the music of Englebert Humperdink. My lover gave up trying to arouse me with her East-European-Gymnast-Tours-A-Corn-Processing-Plant routine.

One Friday afternoon, as I sat reorganizing my collection of Kelly brochures, the telephone rang. I let the answering machine pick it up. At first I didn't believe my ears, but it was a Kelly Boss! I snatched the phone and shouted, "Hello? Hello? I'm Here! I'm ready to work — honest!"

The voice at the other end of the line was curt and business-like, "Listen, we have an assignment here that needs doing and the woman who normally does it had to go out of town. There's no one else around who can do this on such short notice, so I figured I'd give you another chance, even if you don't deserve it."

Instantly my old skepticism returned. "So ... what's the job?"

"Okay, all you have to do is go to an office downtown, listen to the bids people make for some state road projects, write down what you hear, then call a lady in New Jersey and give her the results. Can you do that?"

"Of course. I'm amply qualified for such work. Now, may I inquire as to the rate of pay?" I wasn't screwing around this time.

"For about 30 minutes of work you'll get paid $20. Take it or leave it."

I bummed a ride downtown from a friend and glided up the steps to the bidding office, the invisible hand of Kelly guiding me along the way.

TREVOR RIGLER

Here's A Real Job For You!

Forklift driving is more than just a job, it's an art. My days of forklift driving included many fantasies of racing down the warehouse at full speed and pretending my forklift is the General Lee, sometimes letting out a Yeeee Hawww! A forklift is an indestructible machine, as I found out, you can run into virtually anything without damaging it or yourself.

You supposedly need a license to drive a forklift. This is so the company you slave for doesn't get fucked up the ass when you crash the thing into some acidic chemicals and it melts half of the workers limbs into a nice green sludge. I guess my company didn't care because they let me drive for 3 months before I got a license. The training was the greatest. You got off work for a few hours and got free donuts along with it. The first thing we had to do was view a safety video and then take a test on it. Now, if you've never seen a safety video for a factory job, boy are you missing out. It usually shows some dumb asshole who has no common sense, breaking a leg or so, getting melted by chemicals, or getting a small piece of metal flung into his face taking out his eye. The training video was no exception. Total fucking comedy. It contained many disgruntled forklift operators trucking around causing all sorts of chaos. One guy ran into an unsuspecting office working in the forehead with one of the forks. One thing to remember, office workers are ALWAYS IN THE WAY! They feel as if we have nothing better to do but wait till they finish yapping to each other and move their white collar ass out of the way. When the big wigs were around the plant, my greatest dream was to stick both forks so far up their asses they'd be speaking with a steel tongue, or run them down with a 1500 pound load. "I'm sorry Mr. Big Cheese, I didn't mean to leave tire tracks on your $700 suit."

The video also warned us about driving fast on wet surfaces. Basically, kids, forklift tires have no traction on smooth warehouse floors, so when you are speeding on

Work! Work!

water you start skidding like in a Smokey and the Bandit movie. Pictured in the video was some careless forklift driver, probably thinking about how plastered he was going to get after a hard day of work, speeding around loading barges. Next thing you know, the rug is pulled from the machines and SPLASH! there goes the driver and all right into the fucking drink. Boy, that was funnier than a blind person in a maze. If only I could have gotten a copy of that video. I would have bootlegged the shit out of it.

If you are anything like me and don't care about your job, fuckups can only improve your day. The first day I drove a forklift, I dumped a whole pallet of six $600 stoves right at my boss's feet. I was new then so I was a little scared. After awhile, I became a skillful driver and became more daring. One time I was driving at full speed and made a sharp turn. The whole lift went on two wheels and almost tipped over. I almost shit my pants on that one because I probably would've flew out of the cab and the machine would've crushed the life out of me. That would've sucked.

The beauty of being a forklift driver is you're sitting down and when you

> You supposedly need a license to drive a fork-lift. This is so the company you slave for doesn't get fucked up the ass when you crash the thing into some acidic chemicals and it melts half of the workers limbs into a nice green sludge. I guess my company didn't care . . .

want to slack off you can. When you want to waste some time you can act like you're working by driving around as if you are looking for something. Another good thing is you can ignore people by using the excuse, "Oh, I'm sorry, I didn't hear you, the forklift is too loud." Fucker.

I had only two big accidents while driving. One day I was driving around, half asleep because work started at 6AM, and I slammed right into a plastic wall and took the whole thing out. The fork pierced the wall and white plaster dust blew everywhere. The only problem it caused me was a few days of ridicule and the maintenance guy bitching at me because he had to fix the wall.

Another accident I had was when I ran into a concrete pillar and took off a chunk the size of a football. Every month or so we would get these crates that would come in a truck that was about a foot higher than our dock. This really sucked because when we put up our ramp it made a 45 degree angle. Since the tires had no traction, you had to go up it at full speed and then immediately drop the forks so they wouldn't fuck up the crates. Well, wouldn't you know, speed racer that I am, I went up the ramp and didn't drop the forks in time. Luckily, I did slam on the brakes before I pierced the crates. Oh shit, I thought to myself, I'll have to do it again (this was the fifth or sixth time). Backing up, I turned the wheel and one of the back wheels went up the side of the ramp. A loud bang followed, as I looked behind, a big chunk of concrete fell off the pillar from the truck smashing into it.

Picture it, me about to shit my pants because in one false move the whole forklift was about to tip over, the warehouse manager standing behind me shaking his head, and my coworker busting up laughing and calling me dirty names in Spanish. Boy did I curse his children's children. Not knowing what to do, they old me to jump off the forklift. I responded, "Are you fucking out of your gourd? If I move, this thing will tip." They assured me that wouldn't happen (yeah it was going to crush their heads between metal and rock), so I got off. Fortunately, my skull is still intact and the forklift didn't tip.

Driving a forklift is a perfect way to cost your company a lot of money. By running into things like completed stoves, you ruin the box and sometimes mess up the product. Ramming into walls is definitely a way to give them a heart attack.

I think I cost them the most because one week I forgot to fill a battery with water. This burns out the battery cell. A new cell costs around $1000. As long as you make your mistakes look like mistakes, it won't cost you a red cent. I'm sure glad I didn't have to shell out cash because I'm a poor fucker.

Forklift driving has the advantage of getting good revenge on your company or any of your coworkers. "Oh, sorry Johnny, I didn't mean to crush your foot, but do you got that $50 you owe me?" HA HA HA you stupid fucks. I gave that forklift so much abuse, I'm sure it cost them thousands of dollars. Plus, I was trying to get a new forklift anyway.

SEAN GUILLORY

CHRISTIAN ANGST

Hey, you wacky college graduates...Having difficulty finding employment in the field of your choosing? Remember...Don't overlook the exciting *Service Industry* for challenging lifetime careers a plenty!

Discover the time-tested joys associated with being subservient to pretentious jerks!

Your wine, sir.

What's this crap? I *specifically* requested Boone's Farm Sour Apple!

Discover the time-tested joys associated with being subservient to pretentious jerks!

Hey! It took the waiter *ten seconds* to bring me my drink!

That's it... No tip!

Discover the time-tested joys associated with being subservient to pretentious jerks!

Doesn't our son have the absolute *cutest* spaghetti belch you've ever heard?

Swimming with the Loan Sharks

The company I spent my last assignment at is paranoid and security-conscious, and it should be, it's the people who hassle you when you are late paying your student loans. On my first day I don't have a magnetic security card, and as I loiter in the front of the building trying to get in so I can work, people eye me suspiciously, insert their cards, and slide into the building sideways, afraid that I'll follow them in. No one even says hello. I go around to the loading dock, where a friendly worker in coveralls is wheeling a hand truck full of Coke into the building, and follow him in. I wander around for awhile, scoping out the place. When the Suits find me cooling my heels in the lobby, waiting for my temp assignment to begin, the witch hunt begins before they even say hello:

"Who let you in?"

"I don't know. I just walked in."

"Someone had to let you in. What did they look like? Was it a male or female?"

"I don't know."

My stupid act convinces them that I'll be a good worker, and they issue me a security card and show me to my cubicle. For the next month, for eight hours a day, I'll be entering address changes into the computer so they can track down people who owe on their student loans. I may not enter the addresses accurately, especially if they belong to people I know, but the Suits won't know that until I'm long gone.

The company seems to be concerned about morale because every ten feet or so there are "attitude" posters on the walls:

Together
Everyone
Achieves
More

TEAM and

"It Takes Months to Find a Customer,
Only Seconds to Lose One."

"Let's try to beat that record!" I think, and as I walk past I rip the poster off the wall and stuff it into a convenient paper shredder. I decide that it's my duty to rip at least one of these off the wall every day, and as the days go by I destroy several copies of a long rant about the importance of attitude, written by Christian "inspirational" speaker Chuck Swindoll, and a whole series of Customer Service instructions. There are at least twenty of these; my favorites are #5: "There you go" does not mean "Thank you," and #6: "Uh huh" does not mean "You're welcome."

I cannot believe that normal adults can be surrounded by such patronizing and offensive nonsense and not flee or start smashing things, so my only conclusion is that my coworkers are not normal. If they are, I fear for the future of humankind. The woman in the cubicle next to mine, who spends her day calling people and reminding them that they owe more money, has won many customer service awards; these are not

75

plaques, or anything of value, but grainy xeroxes of xeroxes of forms with her name scribbled in. She has wallpapered her cubicle with these, along with an award for "Best Halloween Drawing." Why not hand out gold stars? I feel like I'm in daycare.

My theory is, even if hell exists, I can't possibly go there when I die because I've already served my time doing Data Entry at places like this. This place has all the standard dehumanizing office features: fluorescent lights that flicker and hum, sealed-in windows that won't open, and a barely working ventilation system that recycles air from 1975. Ah yes, the carpal tunnel syndrome, the death of brain cells, the way coffee becomes the high point of your day ... I'll spare you the ugly details; you've seen it all and you know it's not pretty.

My cubicle is the usual gray coffin, but it has two sanity-saving features: no one can see me when I'm in it, and it has a window. Beyond the parking lot there's a cottonwood tree, a vast field of weeds and wild flowers, rows of corn, tangles of blackberry briars. Green. Sky with clouds and occasional birds. Ah ... I am apparently the only person who has ever actually looked out the window, because when I mention this view to my coworkers they look puzzled. Outside world? Huh? In fact, I develop a running feud with my cubicle-neighbors, who have been office drones for so long that the sunlight irritates them. This simmering unrest goes on all summer, but because they've been trained to fear conflict and they can tell that on this issue I'm unmovable and possibly insane, eventually I win.

I am allowed to take breaks from exactly 10:15 to 10:30, 12:05 to 12:35, and 3:15 to 3:30. I'm out the door and inside the beautiful view before the clock even hits 10:16. Over the weeks I discover that in the half-hour allotted for lunch, if I run as fast as I can, I can reach a creek where a great blue heron, two kingfishers, rabbits and other animals live. On the way I run through the weeds and wild flowers and snatch wild grapes from the vine, and pick catnip and yarrow for tea. When I reach the creek, I crouch on the bank, panting, looking at the birds, digging my fingers into the dirt and remind myself that THIS is the Real World!

I am the only one who has ever seen these animals, the only one who has ever looked at these plants, the only one who doesn't think the land around the office is an empty wasteland. No one else even goes outside for lunch. They prefer the gray cubicle called a lunchroom. When I tell them about the deer or pheasant I saw, about the heron and the grapes and the blackberries, they clearly think I'm delusional. The only world that exists for them is the office; when they look outside they see other offices and other buildings, but I see the spaces between the buildings and the clouds between them.

"VISION" screams the indoctrination poster, with a photo of an intrepid trailblazer standing on a mountain peak. Yet there's not a single employee in the place, from the Suits on down, who would even walk across the parking lot if they didn't have to. Who are they kidding? Anyone taking a look at the brain dead humanoids this company turns people into would know that if you want someone with vision you'd better look at the crazy temp, running across fields cawing madly at crows, entering bad addresses, keeping the window open on the view.

KELLY WINTERS

Ignorant Dumb Shitwork

DAY 1, 12:55 PM

I have just arrived by taxi at the largest building west of the Mississippi River. This is what I have been told at least, although I don't know if I give much of a shit about that. What I do know is that I will be working as a temporary employee for IDS, which stands for Investors Diversified Services, which means absolutely nothing to me. I will sit at a pregnant woman's computer all day and do her work while she lies on her bed at home and waits to spit up her third child in as many years. She produces babies. I produce documents. IDS produces good vibrations and financial services for its clients, so that they may turn the blood of others into money. Things are structured in this way. Everyone is mercilessly happy with the arrangement.

1:05 PM

Bonnie, one of five people who will give me work over the next two and a half months, shows me where the coffee and snack machines are located. She introduces me to people whose names I have forgotten already. She shows me where the door buzzers are located so that I may leave the office at the end of the day. Security, she tells me, has been tightened lately. Evidently, they had a "disgruntled

ex-employee" situation last week, when said ex-employee decided to show up one afternoon and beat the holy shit out of someone. It must have been a marvelous sight, but I only shake my head sadly and mutter something about people not appreciating the wisdom of the world's decision-makers.

1:35 PM

I meet several women in their mid-30's who work in cubicles near me. We are separated by fuzzy office partitions. I make jokes about how we can tie handwritten notes to bricks and lob them over if we need to communicate. They laugh politely and tell me what fun it is to work at IDS. I ask them what they do, and they reply with words like "facilitate" and "consulting director." They use acronyms like "LOE" and "NTR." They frighten me.

2:15 PM

I am now hard at work in my new job. I am surrounded by pictures of young children. The name plate outside my cubicle says "Deb." Other workers in the office walk by from time to time to say, "Hi Deb!" and laugh at the impressive wit they have displayed to the most recent addition to the universe of IDS — I am the "new kid on the block," as they say, and my good cheer must be sought out and nurtured. I laugh, too, and wave back, agreeing to the terms of the contract. It's nice to feel welcome on one's first day at the office. I already feel *like part of the team,* as they say.

I am beginning to get a sense of my importance here — the unarticulated routines that depend on this space being occupied; the necessity of someone being seated in precisely this chair, surrounded by pictures of well scrubbed, white pudgy toddlers, with the name "Deb" fortifying a particular intersection of class status, moral wholesomeness, sexual propriety, good humor and corporate devotion. I have been chosen, miraculously, to safeguard these things. I am a mercenary, a faith healer, a concrete levy called upon to hold back the raging sea of manure that laps through the downtown streets each day, threatening all that which has to do with "Deb." To be selected for such a task! To be plucked from the thicket of all temp workers and given such responsibilities! I am truly humbled, and I wonder if Jesus Christ ever felt this way too.

3:45 PM

I have been assigned to revise a document that outlines the tasks and activities scheduled for a conference in Boston, in early June, 1995. The conference will be attended by IDS "facilitators," as they are called, and will ideally give them some tips on "teamwork" and "the importance of goals" and "satisfaction." This particular document, in fact, pays a good deal of attention to the pursuit of "satisfaction." I sit back and imagine a room in Boston full of satisfied people, eager to spread satisfaction to others, smiling to themselves in satisfied ways, clapping each other on the back, gently touching each others elbows in a way that exudes trust and openess, explaining their satisfaction in great detail — analyzing it, categorizing it, giving flesh to pleasant thoughts, documenting the measurements of success, taking notes on the comforts of others, trading satisfaction like trading cards. At night, they booze it up on expensive gin, smoke fine cigarettes, fuck in moderation on orthopedic mattresses — just enough decadence to maintain that successful, satisfied edge.

3:55 PM

One of the activities scheduled for this conference is a short game called "Mission Impossible." The supplies needed are as follows: bucket, tubing, straps, rope and Koosh ball. I read this and suddenly become aroused.

4:55 PM

I want to continue working until 5:00, but my new friends nudge me gently and tell me that all is well and that I can leave five minutes early with everyone else. I shut down my computer, grab my blazer, and with a modest spring in my step, hit the door buzzer and leave for the day, satisfied with the work I have done so far. Life is so fucking beautiful I can hardly stand to be around myself....

DAY 2, 8:15 AM

There is a young man wandering around in the skyway that connects all the buildings in downtown Minneapolis. On his back he carries a George Jetson type owner pack filled with fresh hot coffee. He darts from passerby to passerby, bragging about all the free coffee he has to give away, screeching at everyone to try a cup. "Who wants coffee?" he asks. "I have free coffee!" he shouts. "Come get your free coffee," he implores. "Yes! Yes! Yes!"

11:35 PM

I look at the books sitting on the bookshelf around the corner from my cubicle: *The Wisdom of Teams,* by Jon R. Katzenbach and Douglas K. Smith; *The Empowered Manager,* by Peter Blacok; *Leading Teams,* by John H. Zenger, Ed Musselwhite, Kathleen Hurson & Craig Perrin. Impressive.

12:35 PM

On my lunch break, I cross the street to the bookstore on 8th and Nicollet. I purchase a copy of Karl Marx's *Das Kapital* and add it to the aforementioned collection of fine reading material.

5:25 PM

I find that I sneer more than usual when I am dressed this way — $85 shoes, $34 slacks, $29 Oxford shirt, $21 tie, $17 belt, $5 boxer shorts, $4 socks, $3 t-shirt. With a minimum of effort and a strategically deployed credit card, I have amplified my position within the coordinates of social power, taking maximum advantage of my whiteness and maleness and carefully supervised middle-class sensibilities. I understand now what it means

Did you ever have the sneaking suspicion that people are laughing at you because you temp?

to be a "fine young man," which is to say that I am no longer suspect. The dollars I spend supply me with credits that I may apply towards the right to act in certain ways. I offer wry smiles to skinny armed men who work at cash registers and have mustaches; at lunch, I bark orders at waitresses and look preoccupied with weighty issues; I wink at the homeless and flip nickels that fall just out of reach of their crusty little paws; on the bus home, I look at the people with nose rings and tattoos and snigger to myself. I am $197 worth of disdain and unalloyed scorn. It is not business attire that I have purchased, but a pair of steel-toed boots.

DAY 3

I spend most of the day putting things into envelopes and routing them to other floors, other buildings, other people. A document and cover letter to Karen D., forms for Phil J. to sign and return, documents to Karen Z. and Tim C., rusty nails and broken glass to Mike R., a bag of splinters to be Fed Exed to Boston, urine and bile samples to Sweden, a ransom note and confidential instructions to a young couple who live outside of Milwaukee, a shipment of arms to the Shining Path rebels in Peru. I whistle as I do this and eat from a plate of nachos left over from a late morning training session. Six hours pass this way and I calculate that in so doing, I have made $57. Before leaving for the day, I grab fourteen packs of Post-It notes and shove them into my pockets.

DAY 4, 8:00 AM

Fridays are "casual days" around here, which means that we are allowed to wear jeans, t-shirts, tennis shoes, athletic socks and so forth — this way, we can all feel free to "let out hair down" as they say, and not be so "uptight." Next week I will smear my clothes with mud and make sure that my face is covered with crumbs and dried vomit before arriving in the morning. I will also show off the track marks on my forearms and the three symmetrical scars running across my left wrist. I have a feeling that people will be most impressed with what a casual guy I can be.

1:45 PM

I have now collated 375 job evaluation packets that Kristen L. will take to Boston next week. Presumably, a room full of employees will circle the words, check boxes, fill in ovals, write anonymous comments, figet, bite their erasers, think naughty things and offer constructive criticism. After the data has been compiled, somebody, somewhere in the country, will be dragged out of bed shortly before dawn, given a blindfold and a cig, tied to a wooden post, and shot through the heart by a motivated and energetic team of sales coordinators.

1:50 PM

Baby break! One of the women on my floor has brought in her 14-month-old daughter for everyone to pinch and prod. This is not the most efficient or productive behavior for a multi-billion dollar corporation to be condoning, but evidently the Baby Break has become something of an accepted ritual around here. One of the cafeteria workers has arrived with a rolling buffet of babies, stacked three feet high and served on a bed of fresh, crisp lettuce, enough for everyone to have at least one for fifteen minutes or so of high intensity play time. "Enjoy your babies," the woman from the cafeteria tells us. "Talk to them! Let them know that someone important has taken an interest! I have decided to select the fattest child available and lecture it on the wisdom of maintaining a disciplined body, free of wrinkles and rolls and mysterious, fleshy pockets where office supplies can be hidden. Oddly enough, despite the apparent distractions, the babies seem to reorient the employees in the direction of particular goals, reminding us obliquely about the necessities of production, disguised in this instance as gurgling, salivating, stumbling cuteness. A clever motivational strategy, I must admit, one that might fare well if adopted on a larger scale by other companies, school systems, government offices and churches. There are, it seems to me, manuals to be written, conferences to be held, ads and strategies to be generated and discussed, medals and plaques and bonuses to be awarded for the most vigorous production of babies. I make note of this and will suggest it to the proper authorities.

4:55 PM

Before leaving the office, I strap a laser printer to my back and smile at the receptionist, wishing her a nice weekend as I buzz myself out the front door.

DAVID NOON

OUR HERO! THE AMERICAN WORKER!
THE TOP 10 REASONS WHY THE AMERICAN WORKER IS SO DAMN STOOOOPID!

Come on, think about it. You know who I'm talking about. The person in the next cubicle or the person shoveling food into his mouth in the breakroom across the table is a damn idiot. You walk into a work place and hope to find a real live fire and brimstone working class person, instead you find Fonzie or Richie Cunningham. You think your boss is your only enemy. You have a lot more to be concerned about because your coworker may be even more dangerous to you. Your coworker gets pissed off, picks up a gun, retuns to work and doesn't shoot the boss, he shoots you. Your coworker rats on you to the boss. He crosses a picket line of his own unions strike. He turns to you and gleefully says, "I'm so excited, Peter Frampton is on tour again." It's enough to make you shit in your pants. But, why is the American worker so damn stooopid. Maybe I can explain. Here's the top 10 reasons why the American worker is the laughing stock of the world.

10) Thinks bosses are ok guys because they pay..
9) Was on break when God was handing out common sense.
8) Cheap beer.
7) Mommy ate acid when she was pregnant.
6) Minimum wage buys a Happy Meal!
5) Being dominated has a certain sexual appeal to it.
4) Can retire after 50 years of work with a pension!
3) Listens to top 40 radio.
2) Fights for flag and country but not for themselves.
1) They are Americans!

IN THE NEXT ISSUE I TELL YOU WHY THE SAVIORS OF THE AMERICAN WORKING CLASS, THE AMERICAN LEFT, IS SO DAMN STOOOOPID!

Spandex Man, The Princess And The Robber

Let's talk about what makes retail jobs hell. Even when they're permanent, they're essentially temp jobs. The turnover is so high that you never know if you'll be out on the street tomorrow, transformed from a clerk to an almighty customer. There are often no benefits, you have to work long hours and weekends, the pay is even lower than at filing jobs, and the public at large thinks you are a stupid, uneducated lowlife if you're taking money instead of spending it.

But as any clerk can tell you, what's worst about retail is the people you have to deal with. Not only do you have moronic bosses to appease, but you're also supposed to suck up to every single person you see, namely The Customers. This means you have to suck up to hundreds, if not thousands, of capricious strangers every day. You need the patience of a saint and the cunning of Satan to endure even the unimaginative jerks who come in.

Then there are the special ones, the ones who have Names. Not the names their mothers gave them, but the ones given to them by the staff. They're famous, but they don't know it. Here are some regulars from my last retail job at a big chain bookstore.

Work!
Work!
Work!

SPANDEX MAN: A 50-ish pervert who'd apparently been in an accident that destroyed all of his brain except the sex part. He'd come swanking in, his thighs sausaged into his trademark lavender Spandex tights, his potbelly encased in a Gold's Gym tank top that set off his furry shoulders. His gold Playboy bunny necklace and other chains clanked as he swiveled his head to ogle all the females in the store. "Do you like this?" he'd say to any female customer, shoving Madonna's *Sex* book in her face. "What are her measurements? Do you KNOW? What are yours? Can I touch you?" One day he made the mistake of hassling a sexy babe in a tight dress. The babe's girlfriend, a diesel dyke with a bad attitude, grabbed him by the chains and told him to bug off. Most days he would squat in the "sex" section of the store, drool over the books, take himself in hand, and disappear into the men's room.

THE PRINCESS: An imperious old lady who'd apparently been royalty in Germany before the war. She'd expect service. Upon entering the store, she'd raise her hand high, snap her fingers and settle with dignity and grace into the nearest chair. "Bring me all ze books you haf on Jungian dream interpretation. Put zem here." She'd make you run back and forth, bringing the books she demanded, until she was walled in. Then, one by one, she'd make you put them back, tapping her tiny foot impatiently. On the rare occasion when she bought a book, she sat on her throne while you went and rung it up. Then you'd return to her to report the total, shine her shoes watch her write the check, go put it in the register, click your heels smartly, return to her with receipt, take the books and put them in a bag, bow and scrape, Ho De Do, carry the books out to her car, escort her out to the car, and salute as she drove away. She could occupy any polite slavish clerk for a good 3 hours. Now, this wouldn't be a problem if she was in a wheelchair, on crutches, or simply infirm — I'd happily give her all the service she needed. But on a lunchtime walk around the ritzy neigh-borhood where the bookstore was located, I saw her out gardening, shoveling up her yard, vigorously digging a hole deep enough to be a grave. Unfortunately, it wasn't hers.

THE BAT MAN: A strange nocturnal creature, who wore a parka with a hood so deep that it was like looking down a stovepipe to see his face. In winter, a permanent shiny crust covered his upper lip. Obsessed with bats, he'd approach, stand inside your aura, and deliver the monologue: "Do you have any books on bats? I love bats. Any book with a bat in it, I'll buy it. I could talk to kids about bats if you want. I have 1,000 books on bats, it's almost like I'm a bat myself .... "

THE LOUD GUY: Before he began to browse, this man would make the rounds and yell at each customer and staff member: "Do you have a COLD? Are you HEALTHY? Not feeling ILL, are you? Your THROAT feel all right?" If he suspected you were harboring any viruses or bacteria, he refused to let you wait on him. One day when he was in my section and had shouted at me once too loudly and once too often, I coughed a vile, phlegmy retching cough, and told him I had pneumonia and was being tested for AIDS. He never yelled at me again.

THE MAD PROFESSOR: A dough faced, intense woman with a thatch of curly graying hair; she peered out through this like a rabid weasel peek-

ing through a hedge. She'd written some Sensitive Books of Poetry and a Sensitive Novel about her affair in a foreign country. She came in regularly to check her sales, which were negligible, and in a rage over this would throw things, screech and carry on. Eventually she became so obnoxious that even the manager didn't want her money any more. He told her to leave, and thinking to spite the store, she never came back.

THE ROBBER: A crazed drifter from California who showed up with a gun one Saturday night at closing time. The reason he got into the store so late was because the manager, whose motto was "Appease all customers even if it costs you your life" insisted that we NOT kick people out at closing time; we were supposed to forget about our friends, families, and suppers waiting at home, and let the customers stay unmolested until midnight if they wanted to. Invariably, these late people didn't buy any books. They simply enjoyed the attention and sense of power they got by keeping twenty ill-paid clerks from going home. We were mere workers, so our free time was in their hands. The

robber, knowing this policy, loitered among the stacks, pretending to browse, until all the other customers had gone home, and then took out his gun. He had the clerks all tied up in the back room, but hung around so long that he was still there by the time the cops sauntered in. He was reading a book at the time. He looked like a customer, and as a customer, he was God and couldn't be wrong. The cops decided he was the one who'd called in the alarm, and that the staff, bound and gagged, were the robbers he had caught.

Fortunately, I had already quit by then.

Every service industry has its regulars, its Famous Names. I've moved since then, have a cushy job that pays a lot, requires no work, and allows me to write my own stuff all day. Still shell shocked, I try not to set foot in stores, as a customer or as a clerk. But friends who work in a local library inform me that the same bunch of crazies come in there, and not only are they first class loons, but they all KNOW EACH OTHER. This is a bad sign. Workers of the world, beware. The Customers are getting Unionized.

KELLY WINTERS

I Work for Boreco INC.

Here I go again. I'm a glutton for punishment. At least that's what people must think. Well, when my money dries up, when the check is no longer in the mail, when I start getting calls from creepy-sounding bill collectors, the only choice is to work. Work anywhere, at any time, doing anything. Low pay, back-breaking nonsensical work for slave-driving bosses. It's all the same to me. It's my life and I deal with it.

My first temp job in Madison was one for the books. I was gleefully told by a local temp agency rep that she had lined me up with a first shift job. BUT, the shift was 6AM to 6PM, three to four days a week. She said, "On the bright side, you'll have 3-4 days off per week and we will increase your pay from $6 an hour to $6.75 an hour if you show up for work everyday." I was overjoyed to hear this. I'd have to get up at 5 in the morning just to get to the job on time and then get home at 7PM, leaving me enough time to scarf some food and go to sleep. It was like having your brain sliced right out of your head. Because to do the job you would have to accept the fact that your life was on hold.

The assignment, or should I say ass-whipping, was at a plastics manufacturing plant 15 miles by car from my home. The plant manufactured plastic molding by use of an injection process. They made a variety of consumer products that people don't need to buy. This included electric toothbrushes, baby ass wipe

PLASTICS ROCK MY WORLD

containers, super balls, reflectors for batteries, medical kits and stuff I couldn't even imagine.

My supervisor greeted me and then took me to the reflector line. A robotic arm deposited row after row of black reflectors on a conveyor belt. My job was to pick the reflectors off the belt and deposit them in a box. I learned the job in ten minutes. Another worker stood close by smiling ear to ear. He looked like he had escaped from a mental ward. He worked the 6PM to 6AM shift. (Imagine the kind of life he had.) His teeth were green and black and his hair was matted down on his head. I could have fried bacon on it. He gave me the low down immediately.

"This is a real brain dead job pal," he told me. "I shouldn't be telling you this but people go crazy in this place. When we get a temp we know he ain't staying for long. Even the one's that do wind up splitting. This one guy was here for 3 months, everything seemed ok and the company was going to give him a full time job. One day he was on his lunch break, he walked out on the floor, grabbed his boom box and walked out a side entrance. We never heard from him again. It was just like that — here and gone at the bat of an eye." He looked at me and started laughing.

After a few hours of work, I couldn't decide if they manufactured plastic or killed brain cells. It was so godawful that I thought they should move the plant to Mexico. Fuck NAFTA, let the Mexicans be bored out of their skulls. With any luck it would save the brain cells of American working dogs so they would have more time to watch prime time sit coms or drink gallons of beer. In fact, I was willing to help them move the machinery to Mexico. Not only was it sensible, it was my patriotic duty!

The reflector job was just one work area. To alleviate the boredom, or to kill even more brain cells, we switched jobs every 6 hours. No matter where you went it was mind numbing shit work.

The afternoon of my first day, I worked on a plastics molding machine called the TM-150G2. The TM became my buddy. I stood next to it, opened a door and placed a metal mold into a slot. When I closed the door, a robotic

ABSTRACT INTELLECTUALISM!

Every so often, I just can't help being crazy. I have to mess with my boss and coworkers. I just can't control myself. One day I was using a ratchet to unscrew a plastic mold. Time after time I inserted the wrench into the mold. I turned to a coworker and said, "This is just like sex, I insert and pull out when I'm done."

My boss overheard me say this and then replied, "You may think you are doing the fucking but you're the one getting fucked."

Then I said, "Oh, so that's why my asshole is torn and bloody after a day of work."

My boss nearly had a shit fit and his eyes bugged out of his head, "What did you say? Now how am I supposed to recommend you for a full time job if you talk like that?"

I answered, "Ok it's torn and bloody but I like it. Does that make you feel better?"

My coworker and I burst into laughter. The bossman shook his head and gave me the evil eye. "I'll have to watch out for you," he said.

(Gee, he was the one who butted in on the conversation. You'd think he would have a sense of humor!)

KEFFO

machine pushed the mold into a hole and then withdrew. It formed electric toothbrush heads. I reached into the machine, took the mold off, placed it in a vise grip and winched the plastic head off the mold. Then I repeated the process. For 6 hours.

The best job by far was sitting in front of a machine that made noises like a grunting pig. It then farted pieces of plastic at me. I cut away the bad parts and put the good parts in a box. I was supposed to watch for nicks and scratches but most of the time I boxed everything.

To make matters worse, the only clock on the plant floor was posted directly in front of me. It was like an extra form of torture watching the hands of the clock go by minute after minute. The only thing to do was ignore it and let your mind wander.

> The best job by far was sitting in front of a machine that made noises like a grunting pig. It then farted pieces of plastic at me.

Most of the time I became part of the machine. I noticed that you could buy yourself time if you used the same body motions. Unfortunately, this meant you were setting yourself up for a lot of aches and pains because your arms and shoulders are not meant to do the same tasks continuously. I simply endured. I had no choice. For me this was a "bridge" job, the kind of job you grinned and bared, to show your next employer that you were a good worker. Based on my previous employment history, I had to begin recreating a work history. For the next 4 months that's what I did.

MY COWORKERS!

In any manufacturing plant the very best part of working is meeting your fellow slaves. I never met such a collection of misfits as I did at Boreco Inc. Some of them tried to assure that the job wasn't so bad. But others had the thousand yard stare, like they'd been in a war. It didn't take long to figure out that Boreco Inc. was a dumping ground for the working class of Wisconsin. No matter what smiley faced spin you put on it, I had seen it all before. Everyone had bills to pay, kids to support, better cars to buy and nowhere else to go. They were going to put in their time and muck through the mess.

In the breakroom, they talked about hopped up cars, said "motherfucker" every other word and pranked each other. I sat back and smiled taking it all in while thinking — so this is what happens to bad boys and girls who don't do well in high school.

To be fair, though, almost everyone I met had an outside interest — some were mechanics on the side, others went to college, one guy was an Olympic class wrestler. The one thing

A temp job working in a plastics factory for $6.75 an hour?

WILL SOMEONE SHOOT ME!

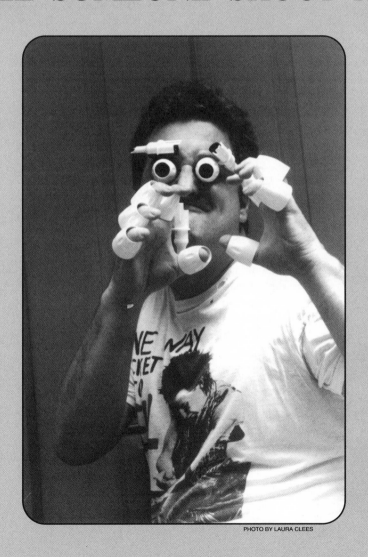

PHOTO BY LAURA CLEES

we all had in common was that we wanted to be somewhere else.

One woman had recently moved to the U.S. from
Russia. I thought all the Russkis were in New York but here
was one in Wisconsin! She turned out to be a great person.
At first she kissed ass to the bosses and I wondered if she
would ever get a clue. Well, that came soon enough because
work, no matter where you work, is still work. She kissed
ass to get a full time job and then made fun of the place in
a hilarious fashion. In her lilting accent she explained her
language difficulties had led to dumb jobs. One time she
went to the wrong company to apply for a job and they
hired her anyway. When she got home and showed her
boyfriend the application he erupted in laughter because
she had gotten a job at a laundry washing company. She
took the job for three days and then quit saying, "What do
you think I'm stupid, Russians don't work like that." I was
the only person in the plant willing to be patient with her
so we became good friends, discussed her life in the former
Soviet Union. She was thrilled to relate how boring and
stupid the bureaucrats were. The clincher was that her
second to last job was as a technician at Chernobyl! Her
father had even designed the damn thing! OUCH! I continually teased her about this.

Thank god for black people too, especially in Wisconsin. One guy named Billy was one of the few blacks who
worked in the plant. He was an imposing figure with a
mouth that ran constantly. One day he stood outside the
plant and threw rocks at birds. Nearby whitebread pig faced
Wisconsin people drove by in their cars. I told Billy that
they would call the cops on him. Billy replied, "I hope
those motherfuckers come for me. At least I won't have to
be here."

Another time I asked Billy if the company had any
decent benefits. He burst into laughter and told me about
the company Christmas party.

"Shit, a few years ago, I went with my wife to the party
and everyone came up to me, pointed at me and said,
'You're Billy right?' Well, it didn't take me long to realize
that since I was the only black guy at the party everyone

knew my name. By the next party they had hired another black guy named Ted. So people came up to me and said, 'Hi Ted.' I just laughed and started drinking heavily. This motherfucking place is unbelievable. I don't kill any brain cells here because I check my brains at the door and collect 'em when I leave."

Another guy totally reaffirmed my pride in the American working class. One week he didn't show up for work, didn't bother to call or make an excuse, and then out of nowhere showed up like nothing happened. Even Boreco Inc. could not tolerate this, they canned him. He smiled and waved goodbye to everyone. What a great guy!

MY BOSS

My boss was the prototype Wisconsin male. He was stocky and squat with a big head resting on his shoulders, topped off with a haircut from hell. He had a German name, too, which was par for the course, because everyone had a German name except for me and Russki woman. He also had the typical Wisconsin accent. Vowels are spoken in a low guttural elongated fashion. You could always tell an outsider from a local this way. The accents sound friendly but you knew that many of them were small minded petty assholes with no redeeming social values. The

absolute worse Wisconsin boss or resident for that matter loved work, loved to drink, they played softball or bowled. They loved to hunt and ice fish and cheer for the Green Bay Packer football team. Like I said, no redeeming social values, especially regarding the Packers!

My boss was not a jerk. He knew the score and was a cool person to shoot the shit with. He encouraged me to stay with the company but knew full well I wasn't a lifer. He already knew that no one stayed at the job and it was his job to evaluate and push new meat into and out of the revolving door. So he never hassled me, admitted to me that the job was a brain stealer and went on his merry way.

He was an excellent mechanic when it came to fixing problems with the robotic equipment. He knew when you were pulling his chain but let you get away with it. One time he told me that he wasn't thrilled about bossing people around. Like many of the production workers, it was just a job for him. He was perhaps the most honest boss I've ever dealt with.

But he also made me very scared sometimes. One day he told me to go to corporate headquarters and apply for a full time job. He wanted me full time. My blood pressure started racing. A full time job working in a plastics

> He already knew that no one stayed at the job and it was his job to evaluate and push new meat into and out of the revolving door.

PEOPLE AND PLASTIC

Plastic is like people. Given the correct care it turns out relatively normal in appearance and serves a function to society. The best plastic is the kind that is sturdy in character, has a clean look to it. It can be counted on for durability and a long shelf life covering food items, adorning cars, homes, and other necessary consumer products.

However, things can go wrong, very wrong. Sometimes during the birthing process the genetic road map gets screwed up and the best laid plans go haywire. In people it leads to mental retardation, birth defects, disease and Temp Slave! readers. But, we do our best to care for the misfits of our society.

Not so with plastic. The pieces of plastic on display came through the birthing process warped and useless. Since they can not benefit society they must be destroyed.

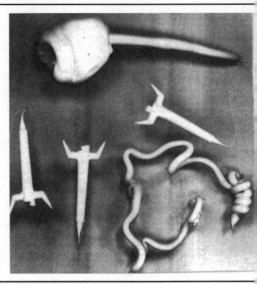

factory for the rest of my fucking life! It was like the devil asking me to sell my soul!

I thought, what the hell, I'll do it just for the entertainment value. No way in hell would they hire me. If they even considered it I'd start messing up the place so they would get rid of me. I didn't realize at the time how desperate they were for workers because days after filling out the application he tried to schedule a physical for me.

STAY IN LINE!

Non-union plant work totally favors the bosses. The noise level makes it nearly impossible to hold a conversation with your coworkers. Because the line never stops you are always isolated. You depend on your coworkers to keep you supplied with tools and boxes. This leads to some heavy shit. Most workers tend to be slackers and you can wind up being screwed.

Sometimes the person who is supposed to relieve you for breaks doesn't show up on time. Since you are tied to the line your first inclination is to blame your coworkers. I saw this happen many times. People just back stabbed the next person to curry favor with the bosses. Every so often my mind would wander and I'd fuck up. One coworker was a Minnie Mouse busybody who ratted me out every time. I wanted to strangle her. But I tend to pity people like her. No matter how much ass kissing she did, it wouldn't get her a raise and she'd be tied to her line like everyone else.

In this respect the anger and frustration toward the bosses is redirected to you coworkers. This plays right into the hands of the bosses. On top of this Boreco Inc. was very good at providing free food every other weekend and this was enough to keep people satisfied.

Every so often, when the lines were down I held court, talked with people about how crappy things were, told them not to be fooled by the feel good nonsense. A few times I hinted at bringing a union in just to piss people off. But they knew, as well as I, that a union would be a waste because no one ever stayed long enough at the job and no one in their right mind would ever want to stay. We joked a lot about it but nothing ever happened.

The hilarious thing was that the workers had the company by the short hairs. It seems like the main requirement for working at Boreco Inc. was that you could count to 5, or had enough fingers on your hand to hold plastic. They didn't even bother to give people benefits to start; they waited until the third month of your employment. It wasn't mean spirited; rather, they just did not want to deal with paperwork. They wanted to see if you would stay before they gave you anything.

Anyway, the bosses are able to keep people in line in a plant situation because of the nature of the work and the nature of the worker. They play worker against worker and the clueless worker falls into the trap. Besides, most plant workers expect nothing, so they demand nothing. It's a scenario that's been played out countless times in plants all over the world.

What working people really need is a sense of themselves as people. Far too often they define themselves by the jobs they do and this makes it difficult to better their lot in life. Respect yourself first and then demand respect from other people, is what I say.

STAGE DOOR LEFT

The bossman was really pressuring me to take a full time job. I put him off for weeks and then had to fess up.

I had applied for another job and miracles of miracles it had come through. I told him I was leaving. (I didn't even bother to call the temp agency.) He was pissed at first but

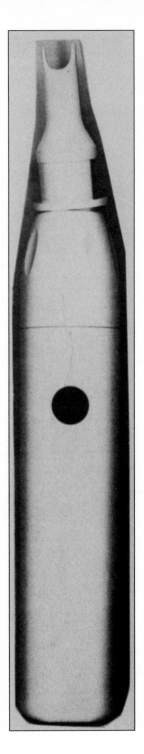

understood where I was coming from. The new job paid double what I was getting with Boreco Inc. He shook his head and said, "Well you gotta go with the money. Good luck."

My coworkers reacted as if a family member had died. To be truthful I felt the same way. They were the nicest people I ever worked with and it was hard saying goodbye to them.

But don't think I'm going soft. My last week of work I packed plastic with gouges in it, if it came out greasy I packed it. I packed the plastic upside down, sideways or whatever way I felt like. Other times I just threw loads into a grinder. It was a last parting shot at the Drudge-masters of Corporate America. The person doing quality control at the company we shipped the plastic to would definitely get the picture once they saw my work. I almost wanted to enclose a big happy face sticker with a booger on it just for the hell of it.

But like I mentioned earlier, this job was a bridge, a stepping stone to better things.

As for the agency, they totally freaked on my boss. They asked him why I didn't contact them and let them knew I was leaving. Of course this was totally ridiculous since I had established my own relationship with my boss and the company. The agency was an afterthought. I only called to lambast them if my check was late. Otherwise they weren't worth a phone call. Besides, they were the fuckers who lined me up with the shit job to begin with. Were they doing me a favor? Was I supposed to kiss their ass for it?

No way. It's just not in my character.

KEFFO

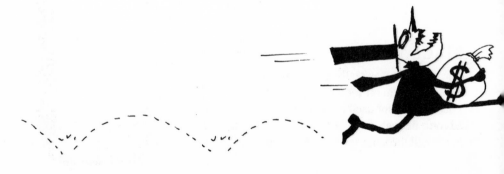

Get Fucked, Bigdaddy!
FEATURING AN OPENLY GAY BOY!

Sitting at my desk at Nations Bank on Thursday afternoon, I started feeling a little depressed because in one more day I would be unemployed again. The department I had been temping for was being eliminated and my job along with it. It was sad because I actually liked my job. The people were cool and the pay was decent. I hadn't gotten a response from any of the 26 resumes I sent out over the past few weeks and it was bothering me. Didn't it matter that I knew every software package known to mankind? Didn't it matter that I had a college degree (even if it was in Piano)? Finally, my office phone started ringing and I answered it. It was my lucky day! One of the temp agencies had found a job that was "perfect for you and your personality." Yeah, like they really know me well enough to take the time to get to know me as a person? I was a money maker for them and nothing more. Hell, they probably thought they could find a perfect mate for me. Shit.

The job turned out to be for one of Atlanta's most successful commercial real estate firms. They needed someone to take over as the office manager while their real manager squeezed out some puppies. The pay would be decent and they would keep me as an assistant when she returned. The office was only a few miles from my home. I would have insurance and it would magically make my life a beautiful scene.

First, I had to be interviewed by three of their executives. I, of course, had to meet the approval of the top dogs and then I could be part of their little hetero-family. I bring up family because this "highly successful company" was little more than a rinky-dink family business. I always thought it would be cool to work for a family business because the people might actually have some depth and personality. I was wasting wishes.

In my first interview, Pigdog (this was the lady whose place I was taking), had to grill me on my computer experience. She wobbled into the office and splurged all over me about how wonderful the company was even though they treated her like shit and abused her. She was convinced it was the job of everyone's dreams. She immediately fell in love with me and knew that I was perfect for the job.

The second interview was even more fun. Buttlick, the VP of the company, put me through a grueling set of personal questions. My favorite was, "Why did you leave your jobs after only a few months?" I furtively tried to explain that the reason they call temp jobs temp jobs is because they are temporary. Hello? Is anyone home?

I somehow managed to impress this guy because I had a degree in piano and "used my talent to glorify the Lord." I wanted to scream out the truth about my church jobs. I was only there for the money. I didn't care about singing hymns and playing that really wretched and foul music. Buttlick wondered why I didn't have a church job anymore. An honest response would have been "I would rather lay down in my own vomit than take part in the hypocritical subculture known as American religion," but I decided to lie instead saying "I just haven't found the right church family yet." I don't know how I said that without hurling all over Buttlick's desk. I could have elaborated, adding, "You know, the kind of church family that accepts us queers ... do you know of any churches like that?"

My final interview was really interesting. BigDaddy, who founded the company, decided to inquire about my own philosophy of life. He informed me that I would have to read the book he recently published about how religion is the only thing that can make a company successful. He wondered,

"Don't you think a man and a woman can have the best kind of relationship?" Well, no, actually, I would rather be with a man. I'm a big gay boy and my husband is going to do me tonight. I didn't say this. I smiled and nodded my head. I assured BigDaddy that I was the heterosexual worker he wanted me to be. I was his hetero-wet dream. I knew then that I was going to have a lot of fun at this job. Maybe more fun than anyplace I've ever worked.

How did I know that three months of fun awaited me? Easy. You see, I'm gay. I can come across really straight (whatever that means) when I really need to have a decent job for awhile. I'm an activist too. I take jobs at fundamentalist companies and totally destroy them from the inside out. It brings me so much joy! A lot of gay people don't understand how I can work for these shit-sucking companies but it is so much fun. The president of the company always wants me to go out with their daughter. (Forget the daughter, dude, don't you have a hot-looking son?) They *love* me! They think I'm an outstanding young Christian boy. Ha! I should have been an actor.

The job was easy. I managed a staff of 6 people. My assistant, Vomit-Wench, was the sister of the president of the company. She was without question one of the least intelligent people I have ever known. She was pitiful and disgracefully stupid. She could however type and being a "family" business she had secure employment. Vomit-Wench never had a clue as to what was going on in the office. She blindly did everything I told her to do. She was a better TEMP SLAVE! than me!

I got to network and made contacts with other real estate agents. The agents of other companies would take me out to lunch and I would give out (for a *free* lunch!) all you might want to know about my right-wing company. I was fucking selling them out! I gave out the client list and met some pretty cool people. (People in the real estate biz, i.e., an agent, etc., are not bright people. They are the kind of people who can't get a college degree so they settle for being a real estate agent. They are Way, Way, *Way* overpaid.)

One of the best things about this job was the postage machine. I had access to all the free postage I wanted. I started sending my friends in Germany, Canada, and Brazil all kinds of cool stuff from the States. I would send whatever I wanted including my significant other's mail. I even sent out a gay newsletter, all of which was paid for by this company that backed the Christian Coalition. It was priceless!

I already had a computer at home with a printer but I needed lots of paper. Since I had my own key to the office, I could get in early and send out all the stuff I wanted. I even mailed the security guards' letters and bills. Since I helped security they never turned me in for carrying loads of mail down to the mail room. The accountants didn't know what was going on. The Prez suspected that one of the agents was using the postage machine. *They never even suspected me.*

I decided that mailing stuff wasn't enough and I needed to call my friends. It didn't matter anymore whether I got caught because I knew I was moving away in two weeks. The worst thing they could do was fire me. Why not make the most of it?

I became friends with the receptionist, TooNice. She was the only person of color at this company and the agents — who were all racist pigs — treated her like dirt. I started giving her 2-3 hour lunch breaks and made VomitWench answer the phone. Oh the joy it brought me! I told VomitWench that I had given TooNice a special project that required her total concentration. VomitWench, who's disgustingly idiotic, believed me. I, of course, made sure that Too-Nice got paid for a full days work.

One of my favorite things that happened was when one of the older farts of the company asked Vomit-Wench to take his clothes to the dry cleaner. *I was appalled.* Even though I didn't like VomitWench I decided it would be more fun to use my power and cause a ruckus. I immediately sent e-mail out to everyone in the company

> BigDaddy . . . informed me that I would have to read the book he recently published about how religion is the only thing that can make a company successful. He wondered, "Don't you think a man and a woman can have the best kind of relationship?" Well, no, actually, I would rather be with a man. I'm a big gay boy and my husband is going to do me tonight.

expressing that the staff of this company did not do laundry and other crap. We did the office work and that was it. The OldFart hit the fucking roof and demanded that I be fired. The prez, who thought I was the greatest thing since candy, refused to fire me. He was proud that I had the guts to stand up for staff (especially since it was for his little spineless sister). I had set a new standard for the staff at this pitiful little company. I was a hero to them.

The head accountant (a complete loser) kept inviting me to play piano at her church. I told her I would be delighted to. I arrived on a chilly Sunday morning and banged my way through a rendition of Tori Amos' "Icicle" and Prince's "Darling Nikki" for the offertory. The younger people in the congregation flipped. This was the Sunday before my last week so I couldn't have cared less about what happened.

The last day was very quiet. I was low key and kept to myself. I stayed at my computer most of the day writing my little "good bye" letter. I fixed it so that the letter would be waiting for everyone on their computer the next Monday morning. The letter basically said that I was a gay activist and that I had totally taken them for a ride. I never heard from them or the agency because we moved that weekend to another state. I know they were screwed because Pig Dog decided not to return to her wonderful job and they would have to train someone all over again. They would probably never trust another temp!

Those idiots probably had the entire building cleaned to rid it of all my germs. Being gay, they probably automatically assumed I put AIDS germs on everything. I remember BigDaddy talking about Greg Louganis and how

HEY, TEMP SLAVES! REMEMBER MINERVA MONERA FROM ISSUE 2? SABOTAGE IS FUN!

"EAT UP THE PRETZELS YOU ROTTEN BOSSES!"
—MINERVA

Greg should have been shot with all the other fags in the world. But BigDaddy didn't know that his favorite employee was a big fag! Why are people so stupid?

A lot of people probably take great offense at what I did. It doesn't matter though. I'm going to do it to every company out there who discriminates against women, blacks, Jews, gays, Native Americans and anyone else. This stupid little company liked me so much that they were going to send me to real estate school. They would have paid all my expenses. Of course, since I'm gay, I am no longer worthy of love. I am something horrible. I am anti-family. Wrong, wrong, wrong. I am anti-discrimination. If you are a company that discriminates, watch out. I'm coming to your little fascist company next.

LITTLE JOE

Building a Fuckin' Parking Garage

I moved to Charleston, South Carolina, in January of 1993. My girlfriend had found a regular job but was waiting for her first payday and we would be broke until then. I had signed with three more temp agencies and had only received three days of work in about a month. By this time it was early February and the cupboards were bare, the rent was due, and we had a quarter tank of gas. My girlfriend's payday was still a week away. I had been putting it off, but on this Friday I was going to have to go to the Industrial Temps building that had a big "SAME DAY PAY" sign out front.

Friday came and I was up at 4:30AM, arriving at the Industrial Temps building by 5:00. As my girlfriend was driving me there I tried to catch a nap and phase out my mind, but I was actually scared of work for the first time — I had heard stories about this place. As I entered the building my first surprise was how cold it was inside. Usually when you enter a building from the winter cold you encounter a blast of heat. At the Industrial Temps building it was almost as cold inside as outside. My second surprise was that I was the only white guy there and the 30 or so people there looked up as I walked in. Now I was really knowing fear! It didn't help that I looked like a skinhead. It was going to be a long day.

I walked up to the counter where men were taking names and giving orders. The counter was so high that it came up to my neck. An old white dude growled at me, "Name?" and I said my name. Then: "Social Security?" and I told him my number. "Go to the window." He was pointing to a window on the other side of the room. After my reeling stagger to the other window ended a guy there asked "Shoe size?" and I said, "Nine and a half." He handed me some size 10 steel-toed wading boots and a hard hat with a bologna sandwich in it. This was great because I hadn't had any breakfast. I guessed that most of us had missed breakfast because everyone was quietly wolfing down their bologna sandwiches.

People kept coming in. Some parked their shopping carts of worldly possessions outside. Some talked about not seeing each other since jail. Two other white guys came in and I felt a little easier. An old skinny black dude sat next to me and introduced himself. I had been there an hour. At 6:00AM the doors were shut and locked. A few minutes later a man came out and gave orders. "When your name is called go out this door and sit down in the van," the man said. "If the assignment doesn't require boots, leave them." The next man said, "Parking Garage." Then he began to read names off a piece of paper on his clipboard. Those called dropped their boots and began to move out the door. My name was called and I left. Outside it was still about 30 degrees and breezy. About 30 to 40 of us piled into a Ford Econoline van. It was packed! It fucking smelled like sweat and bad breath. We were miserable. The other white guys weren't in this van. They were likely going to be wearing wading boots at their assignment. Wading water in 30 degree weather?

We were driven to a parking garage that was being built in downtown Charleston a few blocks from the bay, right next to a hospital. The garage's location by the water made for a nasty

Sidewalk Bubblegum ©1994 Clay Butler

little sea breeze. I was given a hammer and told to go the 4th floor where I would be knocking the wood from the ceiling where the poured cement had not covered the molding.

My first partner was a 20-year-old black dude, of course, that seemed pretty nervous. "These fuckers will work us to death," he said. "We're just like slaves." I agreed. He asked me if I was from California and I said I was. He said it showed and advised me to not let the foreman know, although he figured my accent would probably give me away if I talked too much. We worked slow (I had no idea what the fuck I was doing) and it never warmed up. After about four hours the foreman came over and told my partner to leave. He was fired for talking too much. No pay. No ride home. The foreman warned me about talking and asked me where I was from. I told him. He paired me with the skinny old guy who had sat next to me back at the Industrial Temps building. He was nice and warned me to act like I was working hard and to be quiet. At about that time the foreman heard us talking and told us to be quiet. After that, he referred to me as "faggot" and to my partner—along with other blacks—as "nigger."

I wanted to leave, but I wanted to eat. I stayed. At 11:00AM we got a five minute break. I was tired and needed water. I looked around for a fountain, but there wasn't one. I went back to work and at 2:00PM we got lunch break—30 minutes. I had no food and walked a few blocks to a fast food joint for water. I ran back so I wouldn't be late.

The job dragged on and I got tired and delirious. Reaching above me from a ten foot scaffolding to whack at the wood made my arms so sore that I began to have trouble keeping my arms up. Looking upwards kept me off balance. Finally I weakened and fell off the scaffolding, cutting my arms, back and face. I almost gave up. The foreman was on my ass in a flash. "Get up faggot" he was screaming in my ear. "You're just a pussy from California" and so on. So I climbed back up the scaffolding and kept on whacking at the wood.

No more breaks. More people were being thrown off the job as the day went on and we weren't being told when the job was going to end. Finally, at a little after 6:00 pm, they blew the whistle and shouted we had 10 seconds to get to the van. My partner said, "Move it boy" as he jumped from the scaffolding. "They'll leave you and you won't get your pay." I joined in on the bolt for the stairs.

The ride back to Industrial Temps wasn't as packed as the morning ride —we actually had places to sit. When we arrived we waited about 45 minutes for a check to be issued to us. If we wanted cash we had to wait in another line where they were cashing checks for a five dollar fee. When I walked out of the Industrial Temps building, I had $31. I went straight across the street to a convenience store and bought about $5 in food and drinks. I went to a grassy area just off the concrete fueling area and collapsed. It was the best food I'd ever had. I had a long walk home because my girlfriend had driven the car to work. I just enjoyed being free.

Two months later, Industrial Temps was shut down.

BOB THOMPSON

Hello, My Name Is Temp 378

Temp 378 was my "temporary file name" and serial number at my twelfth temp assignment, here in Portland. I couldn't pass up the opportunity to write an article about the hell I've just passed through when Jeff made me the offer. And why any of this is semi-interesting is because it's all true. And there's nothing more perverse than the truth.

Downtown is the worst part of this city. It's full of yuppies who are snooty and snobby and horrible people. I should have known something was wrong when the agency excitedly called and offered this four-month, $10-an-hour position to me. The only catch was that I had to be interviewed before starting the job. I have since learned never to consent to that again. But with nothing else going for me, I followed orders. Later, I was told that I would be hired, but at the rate of $9 an hour. After meeting me in the flesh, they lowered their price.

On my first day, I walked in and immediately felt a chill in the air. I sat down and was promptly given two Ami Pro software manuals to read. My duties would be typing spreadsheets and financial statements. To my supervisor's amazement, I picked up the software program "very good for someone who was thrown into it cold."

But my supervisor was the cold one. A woman in her fifties, married with no children, she constantly put out a tense vibe every hour of every day, until 5:00PM when I'd literally run out of the office.

Her desk was one foot away from mine. There was hardly any conversation between the two of us. She was silent, except for her constant throat-clearing, which was pretty fucking annoying. Even if she attempted to be nice, she only succeeded in making me feel even more uneasy. We had nothing in common. She was super-conservative, pinched-looking, nunlike, frigidlike, uptight, and one cold fish. I just couldn't do enough to please her. One day, she was out sick and I completed all the assignments. Upon her

Work! Work!

return, however, more work arrived. I let her know that when I left the previous day, the In Box was empty. She haughtily replied, "Well, now it isn't."

I'm always thrown into temp situations with difficult personality types. She was my biggest problem. Around her, the tension was so thick that you could cut it with a knife. She'd give me her evil eye every morning when I got in, with an extremely fake-sounding "Good Morning." She'd call her friends on the phone and talk about nothing and emit the most sadistic, sinister laugh I have ever heard in my life. For after-hours fun, she played racquetball. Her husband's name was Leighton. Phony and narrow-minded. I hated her guts. But I tried to be my sweetest self, sometimes even cracking jokes. There was only silence, on her part. I was rebuffed, totally snubbed. She had seen Jim (*Answer Me*...ed) mentioned negatively in a local rag, and was, of course, offended. She wouldn't offer any kind of valid opinion to me about it, except to off-handedly and unexpectedly state that she saw his name in the newspaper. She then curtly asked, "So, what does your husband write about?" "He writes about bashing in the heads of scum like you," I wanted to answer, but I was discreet and humbly replied that he writes about current events, including

106

a book about working-class people in this country. Her face registered no emotion.

There were other morons there, as well. On one of my first days in the office, I happened to take a different route, and I passed by one of the secretaries. She turned to me and yelled out, "SPY." I had no idea what she was talking about and I didn't answer her, but I wondered how I, a mere temp worker could be a spy for anybody. I always feel like I'm the one being watched. Later, I mentioned this incident to a couple of people, and they all instantly knew whom I was talking about. "She's done the same thing to others," they replied. "She's just a little moody."

I'd come in at 8AM and say hi to my fellow staff, and they usually wouldn't respond. They'd look at me and sigh. They probably thought of me as a weirdo who wears black and never smiles: a scary person. With my frizzy hair, heavy Brooklyn accent, odd punk-rocker from the seventies look, yes, I'm different. And to most people, different equals bad. Anything that's a little different is "oddball." They don't understand it; they don't want to understand it; they're frightened by it, and therefore shocked by it. God forbid the days when I'd wear my butterfly or leopard-skin pantyhose to work. Mere stockings, which are sold in stores, for Christ's sake. But you wouldn't believe the looks I got. It was like I was from another planet.

After working there over three months, I left a note for one of the big shots that I'd send his fax, but I needed a phone number for it. He tossed the papers on my desk and hurried away. I remained calm, however, and wrote him a courteous note explaining, "I'd be happy to fax this for you, but I need the fax number." I signed my name. He turned to me and in a condescending tone asked, "Is this you?" Like he didn't know that I'm Debbie. Maybe I should have signed it, Temp 378.

Whenever people came into the office, everyone was introduced, except me. I was there physically, but I was treated like a non-person. Even though I did a huge chunk of their work, I didn't exist. In their eyes, I wasn't really there.

Christmas came, and not even a thank you. They threw a Friday lunchtime pizza party and I made the mistake of attending. As soon as I entered the room, it got tense. I felt so uncomfortable around these stiffs that I pretty much ate my lousy piece of pizza and walked out. Later that same day, I finished all my work and split at 5 to 5. On my way out, I said to one of the secretaries, "Have a nice weekend," and her witchlike response was, "Is it 5:00?" According to my watch it was.

Riding the bus to work was no better. I would sometimes get on the wrong bus, accidently, because I was just trying so hard to get away from the herd of sheep at the bus stop. People on the bus were ugly, too. Elephants used to sit next to me and completely take over. Once, a woman got on who

started fidgeting badly, and then she took out her PacifiCorp health insurance packet and started thumbing through that. I thought to myself, how a few months earlier, I had worked as a temp at PacifiCorp, and the rejection I felt that day. I took a glimpse at this "woman." She wasn't human. To me, she was a robot. And that's why she got the job.

To ease my woes, I brought in a radio and listened to the oldies station. I'd always turn it to Neil Diamond, The Mamas and the Papas, Grace Slick wailing "Somebody to Love," and Eric Burden. I put two pictures of Igor, my fourteen-month-old pug pup on my

computer. You would think that these shots would be an icebreaker, but people acted like the photos weren't even there.

They talked to me only if they needed something. The accountants would walk past my cubicle, stare at me, mumble inaudibly, and sometimes even look at me and laugh. I call that down and out rude. But if I tried to make eye contact, they'd look away. I guess this is some kind of game they enjoyed playing. They were in their own worlds and slaves to their jobs. They have coffee mugs with slogans like, *He Who Dies With the Most Toys Wins.*

I have a pretty good sense of detecting bullshit. I didn't like their crap and I wasn't going to take it. I'd reciprocate by giving them the finger behind their backs, sneering at them, sticking out my tongue at them, making faces, calling them dicks, and calling them cunts. I guess that I make friends wherever I go.

But actually there were a couple of OK people there. The receptionist was interesting. She was into spirituality, the hereafter, and admitted to me that her husband was bipolar, and that she had him arrested for domestic violence, but that she still loved him. A mail clerk there agreed with me that it was an evil place, the people sucked, and that he felt their negative vibes, too.

> Whenever people came into the office, everyone was introduced, except me. I was there physically, but I was treated like a non-person. Even though I did a huge chunk of their work, I didn't exist. In their eyes, I wasn't really there.

I can't figure out these office types. I'd come home from work and feel so sad and mad that I'd actually cry. These pieces of human feces made me weep. Well, nobody fucks with me and gets away with it. Instead of whining about it, all I can do is expose it. These monsters are boring, stuck-up drones. They probably called me white trash behind my back. But they have absolutely nothing to offer in their life-times. They have a stinking day job where they feel important, and then they go home to their bland family and get pussy-whipped and yelled at all night. Nobody will remember them after they die. They're very bad people.

I know I'm a good person.

I'm an outstanding worker and by right, bosses should be bidding for my services. I have twenty years secre-tarial experience, know most of the software programs, can type 80 wpm, I'm accurate, and I'm always on time. But still, I can't get a permanent job.

One day, I'm gong to win and they're all going to lose, I just know it. My spirit and energy are stronger than theirs and they resent me for it. I was so pissed off, that for a while I made my screen saver read, *He Who Laughs Last, Laughs Best*. No comment, on their parts.

My last day there felt the same as my first. The supervisor squeezed as much work out of me as she could. They gave me a small bouquet of carnations with the note, "Thanks for all your help." I split with my flowers into the cold night air. There was a sad-ness to it, which only I felt. I left four months of my soul in that place. Now I have to hope for a new job and pray that somebody else will hire me. Pretty soon, I'll run out of places to work in this city. I'm registered with fifteen temporary agencies. It's like playing the slots in Vegas. They constantly call me, sounding like used-car salesmen. "I know I'll get you that perfect job and soon," they promise me.

So much in life is temporary.

DEBBIE GOAD

A More Perfect Victim

I'm yours, if you can meet my price.

The phone rings: we talk terms, specifications, qualifications. Can I do this? Would I do that? We reach an agreement. I pride myself on being prompt and professional. Tell me what you want — you're the boss. I've been doing this since I moved to town six months ago. Started working my third day here.

Yeah, I'm an office temp. But please don't tell my parents, they think I'm a successful cocktail waitress.

I offer technical support for agencies, corporations, offices, conventions, and showrooms.

I had met the man my story centers on before. He was a CEO waiting in the VIP lounge before being ushered into the standard mid-level executive offices: a closed space, a little womb, a carpeted and couched pseudo-cunt of tomblike silences. He'd struck me as a specimen of the wealthy, pampered man of upper-class origins and Eastern college affections.

After "servicing and supporting business professionals" for six months, I quit. I'd been slaving for people whom I'd normally cross the street to avoid. I had put in my time, made my contacts, worked hard, and discovered that virtue is its own reward. That's it. Let me repeat myself — virtue is its own reward. Kinda makes the sound of one hand clapping. So I quit. One day I was there, and the next my high-heeled secretarial-style shoes just kept walkin'. I wanted a job with more. More money, more creativity, more power, more perks. A career wherein if you worked hard and you worked well — well, your work would be rewarded. I investigated different business opportunities, all good growth industries. After examining my vocational strengths I found a place where I could utilize my Bachelor of Science degree. A job where I could employ my people skills while earning a good salary and breathtaking perks. In short, I found a position in a brothel.

110

When I'd been toiling in the fields of lust for a week I took some of the wages of sin and went shopping. Barneys, Kamali, Donna Karen, Armani, Victoria's Secret, Sax's. A paradox: when I was poor I'd dress cheaply, which often comes out looking trashy (in every sense of the word), but now that I had come into richness I adopted an expensive look.

I'd been working at the brothel for a month when I met him again. Our glances click and the attraction is immediate. And mutual. I recognize that haughty reserve and impeccable tailoring from my stint as a working girl. I mean the temporary support kind. And the guy doesn't recognize me in my new Uptown persona. The last time we'd met I'd been clothed in Lerner's and coifed by Command Performance. As I sneak surreptitious glances I wonder if there's ever been anything that he's wanted that he hasn't gotten ... immediately.

We're alone in The Master's bedroom. He provides the outlines of our little psycho-drama.

He's been a very, very, very naughty tool of the capitalist class and betrayed the principles of his youthful idealism. He's sold empty dreams and vapid values to a nation as they sat mesmerized in front of the electronic hearth, the cathode snake coiling around the collective soul. He fears he'll continue in his wayward wickedness. He wants to be good, really he does, but he just can't stop the dream machine of the advertising agency and PR firm that bear his name. Oh, Mama, can this really be the end? To be stuck inside a whorehouse with the advertising blues again? He wants me to be his twelfth-grade teacher, Mrs. Busby, the woman he wanted to butt-fuck over the anatomy dissection tables, and whose thwarting of his desires has proven to be the fuel that powered his rocket flight to wealth and power, always hoping to take, to buy, to own the elusive Mrs. Busby, whose rounded, protruding and oh-so-succulent caboose (in her oh-so-chaste dress and sweater sets), was always in evidence and on his mind. She, and her denial of his boyish enthusiasm to sodomize her, fixated him and set his future course: she was the cause of his needing to stick-it-to the public. His destiny, he's always felt, was to be a poor poet, but thanks to a run-in with a close-thighed, cashmere-ensconced mother-figure, his life has been subverted from its natural course and he's been forced to butt-fuck the id via air-brushed images. Ah, it's enough to make Freud weep! "The heart wants what the heart wants," he says sadly, tugging at my heart strings. He hangs his head with an appealingly boyish air, but his manhood, having a head of its own, is still hard and tumescent and proud.

I disappear inside the walk-in closet and emerge transfigured in a pale pink cashmere skirt and sweater, pearls, wedding band, glasses, hair pulled high. I carry a slideruler in a menacing manner. I bend over the desk, displaying the globe, to best advantage. The globe on the desk, that is.

He watches.

111

He approaches. His walk, manner, expression — he's regressed to the bashful teen.

Two impulses war inside my breast. One feels compassion for this man who has been thwarted so early in his love resume. The over-riding emotion is to whomp him.

I give in to my baser instincts.

With a vengeance.

Mister CEO is on the table hog-tied, gagged, and naked as a politician's motive.

I decide to start gently, until he gets to know and trust me. I employ the cat-o-nine tails, candles, a cock-ring, riding crop, nipple clamps and a length of cut-off garden hose. I finish with three pool balls in a sock.

"This is just the foreplay, I have even sweeter pleasures in store for you. For one week, starting Monday, you're to be at my beck and call. Work, family, responsibilities — I don't want to know."

"You're too good to be true," he whispers.

I duck my head, not out of modesty, but to count the bills he's left on the dresser. He's dismissed. His tall, broad-shouldered, Armani-clad figure disappears into the night.

On Monday morning he comes into the office I've borrowed from a friend — on the condition that I do her work for a week (calling myself a freelance consultant) while she catches up on Stephen King novels and does the "Week Home Spa to a Younger and Healthier You" clipped out of *Cosmopolitan*.

The clock strikes four minutes after the hour. I nail him to the spot with a glance and then look fixedly at the clock. "I'm sorry," he stammers, reddening in his Roger's Second Time 'Round suit. "I didn't know that the bus ... "

"Spare me the narrative," I interrupt. "Not that I don't care about your commute." Clearly communicating that I don't. "Let's get to work."

"Thank you, mistress," says the Slave, sighing with relief that he hasn't incurred my disfavor.

I let him savor the moment.

"And don't call me Mistress," I yell, glaring over the top of my glasses.

"What should I call you?"

I sigh. Roll my eyes heavenward, as if to ask for divine guidance.

"You may call me by my name," I solemnly intone.

"Thank you Mistre ... er ... Ms. Jones."

"Indeed," I mutter darkly. My exterior verges on the dour, but inwardly I'm excited. I'm planning moves, strategy, scrimmages. Let the games begin!

"What do I do now, Mistre ... oops, Ms. Jones?" pants my eager Slave.

I lead him to the reception area. I hear him moan with pleasure.

"A small windowless room, lit by florescent lighting, painted institutional beige. How did you know?" He beams at me.

"It's my job," I say sternly. "Do you know how to operate a switchboard?" I ask rhetorically, knowing in advance that he won't. It isn't one of the skills

A temp job working for a gun manufacturer
for $7 an hour? Of course I'll do it!
I'm already locked and loaded,
er, um, ahem, . . . ah
ready to start tomorrow!

that come with a privileged background. It's useful.

"No," whispers Slave, eyes downcast.

"There's nothing to it," I lie, wetting my lips with my little pink tongue.

I show him the system. When he's completely lost and flustered and the switchboard resembles the instrument panel of a small commuter plane (but with more lights), I sail back to my office with a cheerful, "Good, you've got it." Got it? He doesn't have a clue, let alone get the hang of it.

It gets better. He doesn't know how to take messages quickly (he barely manages slowly), a UPS person wants a signature, and a very pregnant woman wants the bathroom key. Then, and only then, do I hand him a letter and the phone book and ask him to do a mail merge. "When you have time, of course," I purr, flicking my tail beneath my simple black skirt, my blazer straining across my heaving bosom. "We'll also need the itinerary for the conference in Geneva next week. I'm telling you this to make you feel part of the team, your contribution's important," I say, struggling to maintain a straight face. "This isn't just a meaningless chore, it's a necessary one. Work on it between calls. That way you won't be bored."

"No sweat," Slave gulps, as in fact sweat is starting to wet his cheap shirt. I bet those tender little hairs on the back of his neck are standing on end.

As I leave the reception area, I hear him moan with pleasure.

I go back to my office and a quarter of an hour later I'm back, and the status quo is pretty much the same except that between trying to field phone calls that come in at a rate of eighty an hour, Slave is checking out the computer manual, trying to figure out how to do the mail merge.

"How's the mailing coming along?" I ask, even though the manual's plainly in view on his lap. A bicycle messenger — there for a pick up — doesn't have time to wait for a receptionist and messes with Slave's mind, and then, on cue, I drop off three documents to be faxed, explaining how to run a fax (by the time I'm done with my polysyllabic story the poor guy's ranting and using pink message pads to scribble reminders to said instructions). The phone lines are lit up with incoming calls. I inquire after the mail merge. I drop off a pile of Xeroxing for him to do "in your spare time." The Slave sighs happily. When he asks," May I go to the facilities?" I pretend annoyance. "Can't you wait until your fifteen minute break in forty-five minutes? That's when the floater comes by. You can't just leave the switchboard. There are four calls waiting to be answered NOW."

I strut back to my office in black patent-leather pumps. Closing the door, I file and paint my nails. "The better to draw blood, my dear," I cackle to myself, admiring the red satin slashes across my fingertips.

Slave's really relieved for his fifteen minute break. It's a law, you know, they get two fifteen minute breaks and

114

a half hour lunch (off the clock). For break, Slave goes to the men's room, then grabs a coffee and package of miniature donuts. Thus fortified, he goes back to the switchboard, the memo, the mail merge, the Xerox, the fax, the mail delivery, the lunch order, the UPS liaison, the travel reservations, the data entry, and the restroom key dispension.

His jacket is off and his tie askew when I leave for my luncheon. I let him work an extra half hour on the mail merge before he's allowed to visit Phrank's Frank Cart.

When he gets back I stare at Slave sternly and ask in my best dominatrix tones, "And how is that mail coming?"

I wait until Slave's at the threshold, he's almost there — and then I lick and stamp his envelope. With the switchboard lighting up with disgruntled callers who have been trying, with varying degrees of success, to get through all day, I saunter up to my victim, and drawing myself up to full height I say, "Bring me a cup of coffee, medium milk, two teaspoons sugar. When you get the chance ... "

"No! I will not! You ... you've gone too far! I told you when we began ... I have my ... limits. There are some things I *will not do.*"

"What did you say to me?" I ask softly.

Slave's big eyelashes flutter, his hazel eyes fill with tears. His sensitive lower lip trembles as he begs, "I'm sorry Mistress ... Ms. Jones, but I don't — I don't do coffee. But I'll do any-

thing else you want! But please don't make me get the coffee. I can't. I won't! It ... it goes back to a childhood trauma, something to do with my mother and the beautiful Creole parlor maid and a samovar and a scalding pot of ... Just please don't make me get the coffee!"

"Hello, is there a problem here? It's medium milk and two teaspoons sugar."

"No one else has to get coffee."

Slowly, and with feeling this time, "medium milk and two sugars."

"No one's ever talked to me this way before."

"And you love it! Now you miserable worm, get my coffee ... At your leisure, of course." I glance markedly at my watch. I make a brief note in my notebook. "Then you'll finish the mailing and lick all the envelopes, no wetting stone for you, you bad boy! You have fallen into disfavor. But there are ways of redeeming yourself. By proving you have the right attitude. Do you know what I mean?" I smile cruelly.

"I think I do," Slave gulps.

"Good. Then you can work late tonight on the sales statistics for the last quarter? I don't think we'll be here much after seven, eight at the latest."

"Thank you for this opportunity, Ms. Jones. You won't be sorry."

That was eight months ago.

I work with Slave as my private client during the day and at the brothel at night.

If you're in the Financial District and recognize us, be discreet.

DEW U. CARE

115

TeMp sLAve! hOUsE oF HOrRoR TrADiNg CaRDs

Plastics Make Me Brain Feel Funny

TRAFFIC COP ON ROAD

THE EVIL RECEPTIONIST

I fraid of Bossman. He evil 666.

OHH NO! WORKER RUN AMOK!

BIG BOSS. LITTLE DICK.

HAPPY TEMP INC.   666
666 SATAN ST.
Lucifer, USA 666666   ----------1995
PAY TO THE ORDER OF_____kEFfo_____
_____Dollars
MEMO_____

THE STONED
CO-WORKER

LUNCH TIME!

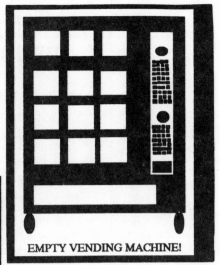

EMPTY VENDING MACHINE!

GIFT OF THE GODS!

INJURY !

WHERE'S THE TOILET PAPER!?!

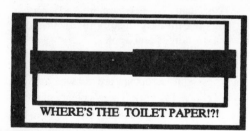

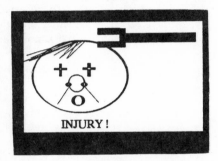

QUITTING TIME!
IS DRINKING TIME!

My First Job in France

RANDOM THOUGHTS

First temp agency I applied to was Manpower in Ohio. They dealt primarily with factory help. Although I had worked in factories, they had no work for me.

I now live in an apartment rented from the French subsidiary of Manpower in Paris, France.

Temp work, per se, is not available to Americans living in France, unless they have been here a long time and have a French spouse and full papers — not easy to get.

To be a worker here, such as working in a factory or at the scrap metal yard next to where I live, is not shameful here. Recently, when French women were asked what profession they'd like their potential dream lover to hold, many said, "worker." To get your hands dirty and to have to wear overalls and to not have much of a future except to continue to be a "worker" is considered okay here, not bad or dead end. But the whole attitude toward work and everyday life here in France is very, very different from those attitudes found in America. France has nothing in common with America. Americans who come here and expect certain things are quickly disappointed. France and America = oranges and apples.

Work!

Work!

Most of the European countries have joined to form a Union of countries. Non-Europeans are not welcome, and are generally not allowed to work. There's plenty of protectionism, racism and isolationism going on. I seldom hear about the United States — Americans are of little concern to the people. I live in a region of France where there are lots of Arabs, and they tend to be unusually warm, open and direct. They always ask me if I am English or German and are truly amazed when I say I'm American. I am the only American for kilometers around, I think.

Americans have the right to stay in France for up to 90

days and after that, you're an illegal immigrant unless you've begun the discouraging process of getting permission to stay here. Even then, you have no right to work. Off the books jobs don't exist here, as we Americans know them. The French are too afraid of fines and punishment to risk hiring people off the books. Unemployment is over 11% so there are plenty of workers willing to work at "niveau SMIC," which is French minimum wage. That comes to around $6 an hour.

I got married to a French citizen just before my 90-day visiting period was up. We had to go immediately to immigration, or I'd be deported. I was technically homeless, so I had to get my husband's parents to formally swear I lived with them and they supported me. I am almost 40-years-old, so this was kind of humiliating, even if it was basically true.

I was lied to and told I had no right to work until after a year of marriage. I started looking for a job right away, anyhow. I barely spoke French. I couldn't even find a dishwashing or babysitting job. Eventually, I found a possible spot in an American style restaurant. They had to write me a formal letter, saying they wanted to hire me. I took that letter to the authorities and applied for a work permit, then waited. Only by marriage to a French citizen did I have a slim chance. I had to pay about $200 for a physical exam. If I had been sick or HIV positive, I would have been deported. I had to wait a year and pay several hundred dollars more to get a French green card, which is only good for a year anyway. I just have to pray they convert it to a 10 year status soon. Then, I can work without prior permission. I hope.

I got a work permit, but only to work in that one restaurant. I prayed the job was still open. It wasn't — but they needed a DJ and were willing to take the chance that the work permit, which allowed me to be a "barman," would also allow me to play records and videos for the customers while they were paying too much for American style food and cocktails.

The employer explained nothing to me about compensation. I was shown a contract, in French, and reluctantly signed it. It gave them the right to fire me on the spot for the first 30 days of my employment. If they wished to renew this 30 day trial period one time, they had to notify me in advance by registered mail. They didn't bother. They forced me to sign another contract in the second month there. It gave them the right to fire me at will, which they did in my fifth week of work. It took me a long time to get paid, and to be reimbursed 50% for my bus/subway pass.

Most of the restaurant workers were students. Students can pay about $200 and work up to three months at a time here, if they meet certain conditions. Employers love the steady flow of slaves willing to take minimum wage. No one fights abuse, since they won't be staying long. When your three months are up, you have to wait a long time (possibly a year) before you can

A REALLY BAD DAY AT WORK

get a work permit again.

I worked six nights a week. I could eat a depressing meal with my co-workers, if I dared. The food was very bad and always made me sick and I have a strong stomach. Management told us the food was free, but we were charged for it. When I wrote to the management by registered mail with a list of questions about my pay stub, things started to go very bad for me at the job.

In France, you are paid only once a month and never in the month you've worked. It's bewildering. You lose about 22% of your pay to taxes and everything you buy has a %25 value-added tax as part of the price. That's why a grocery store chicken can cost you $10, a pack of cigarettes $4. The average French worker is lucky to pull in $10,000 a year. Rents are high — at least $1000 a month — and you must sign a three year lease that you can't get out of. Families lived cramped together, locked in a cycle of poverty. Most people never own their home or apartment here, despite the very sluggish, seller-motivated real estate market.

Most French people move only once in their lives and change jobs only a couple of times. American mobility is so bewildering to them, they often do not believe me when I describe my lifestyle in the U.S. They are astonished I left home in the Midwest at 18, financed my own education, moved to New York alone and have had three husbands and at least 30 jobs. Most French are born and raised in one place. It is nearly impossible for them to qualify for college, and 50% of all first year students fail anyway. Student workers can get training spots for 3-6 months at a time and it is forbidden for them to earn more than $300 a month in these jobs. You meet a lot of 20-year-old married students who still depend on their families. Students here often foolishly believe they'll get a good job with their educa-

tions, when in fact, they'll just enter the ranks of workers glad to have beaten out the other 1,000 clawing for the spot, and they'll probably earn less than $1000 a month for a very, very long work week.

On job interviews, you are routinely asked your age, marital status, number of kids, and how you'll get to work. Ads openly insist you send a photo of yourself and also specify the age groups they are looking for in their applicants. Women are paid less than men but there is a little more equality in pay — everyone earns nothing!

French public transportation shuts down from midnight until dawn. I was expected to work until 1, 2 or even 3 or 4AM at the restaurant as needed. How was I supposed to get home? I barely spoke French and had a hard time finding my way around. I was a

New Yorker for 17 years and am not easily intimidated, but at my horrible job, I felt like I was less than zero. The heat and cigarette smoke was unbearable. No scheduled breaks. The noise was literally deafening and I had to stand all the time. Worse, the staff was made to dance to music from "Grease" and other horrible movies for the clients. We had to drop everything and jump on the tables and perform like monkeys. You had to be very physically fit and pray you wouldn't fall.

The managers yelled at the staff and threatened them. One manager was a gay male who'd been fired from EuroDisney for being homosexual. He was the worst of them — a real backstabber. At 21, he already looked more than 10 years older than he was. Another manager was a dyke from Australia who seemed to like me. I was originally a lesbian, so knew right away what was going on when she stared at my cleavage. She slobbered.

A bright spot was when clients would get up and run out without paying their bills while we were dancing for them. A Bloody Mary was $10 and a pizza was $25, so you can imagine the bills. The wait-person was held responsible for the bill but usually just laughed it off. What were we supposed to do? Work as a security guard while you're standing on a bar shaking your ass?

One night, the dyke screamed at me for no reason. I screamed back and she threw me out. That was that. I cried and cried. I was in a severe clinical depression for about 6 months after that but had no idea how to get or pay for medical help.

Much later, I went on a job interview and kind of pressured them into hiring me by yessing them to death and offering to work in the first month for free. I worked from 9AM until 7PM with no break on a busy trading floor for a small, clandestine brokerage firm. I analyzed foreign currency transactions, ran the back office, was the only secretary for the place, cleaned the kitchen, cooked lunch, shopped, went to the post office, bought bread, etc. ... They did pay for my bus and subway ticket but at the end of the month I got about $600. They talked me into signing a part-time work contract, promising to pay me the difference in cash, tax free. They've never paid me for all the hours I've worked, and the free lunches they promised were inedible and then stopped completely. I now work from 10 to 6, no break, and try to think of ways not to work, steal postage, phone calls, faxes, and something to eat. During the strikes in France last year, I could not get to work for three weeks. They called me and threatened to fire me for refusing to walk 25 miles to work while the whole country was shut down. (You couldn't even buy a newspaper or get mail.) I was not paid for my days at home.

If I want to quit, I must notify them by registered mail and give them 30 days to replace me. I'd like to see where they'll find someone with 15 years of experience in Wall Street, an MBA, who types 110 words per minute on French or european or telex machines, who speaks and writes fluent English plus French and Italian, and who serves coffee. But that's besides the point.

If you've heard France is an easy ride — lots of vacation time, job security through work contract, good retirements, daycare, health benefits — you're just not well informed. France is very socialist/communist/worker oriented. Communism is loved here because it gave the workers the rights they do have. The bosses are bogged down by an impossible bureaucracy. The economy is stubbornly stagnant. Workers play sullen games, knowing they will never get a raise. There are no social benefits for non-workers and non-Europeans. If you quit your intolerable job, can't find another and become homeless, God help you. There are no homeless shelters here. There are no social benefits for those who have slipped between the cracks. You must carry identification at all times, show it on demand, and are usually under camera surveillance. People just submit to this like sheep. Apathy and corruption rule. More than 50% of teenagers here are sexually active and don't use condoms. France has the highest rate of AIDS in all of Europe and almost in all the world.

Later this year, I hope to finally qualify for work at temp agencies. I have no idea what to expect. I'll let you know.

LISA "BIKINI GIRL" FALOUR

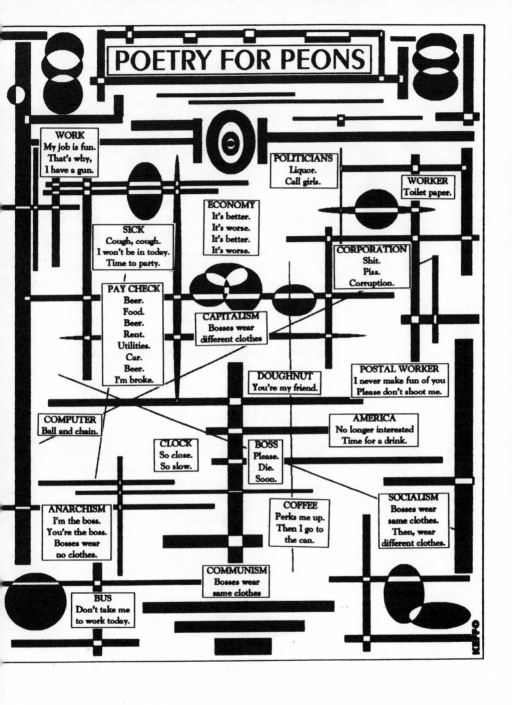

My First Temp Job

I became a temp for typical reasons: I had lost my job through a murky process of quitting/getting fired, and I needed work immediately. I said yes to the first position my temp agency found me, a gig with a dental insurance company.

At 8:00 on a Monday morning I took the #86 bus to the end of the line, where a green shuttle van whisked me 100 or so feet from the bus stop to the historic Shrafft's building in Somerville, Mass. The building was once a candy factory. On the first floor by the elevators and in the cafeteria there were nostalgic black and white pictures of happy ladies selling candy, and factory machines hard at work.

I took the elevator to the fifth floor where a gray receptionist in a homemade cardigan instructed me to wait for a personnel supervisor. While I was waiting, smiley people in business clothing wished me a good morning as they passed the reception area. I was floored; this never happened at my old job. I had been the low woman on the totem pole at a law office where at least three stressful screw-ups, that were my fault, happened every single day. I had a bottle of Pepto-Bismol in my desk drawer that I imbibed daily, and at least once a week one of my bosses made me cry. This kind of smiley courtesy was completely alien to me.

I was directed to a cubicle where a smiling, pregnant woman waited for me. Her name was Karen, she apologized for having kept me waiting, and after a brief overview of the cubicle introduced me to everyone in the company. I followed her around the maze of carpet-covered cubicle walls and sheepishly introduced myself to everyone Karen brought me to. She even introduced me to the president of the company, who she called by first name only. There were no totem poles here, she explained, everyone treated each other as equals. She was a temp who had been hired on permanently, and I was replacing her as temporary marketing secretary.

124

A temp job working in a wind tunnel for $5.25 an hour?

FUCK THAT!
I'LL DO IT FOR FREE!

This was in sharp contrast to the law office I had left, where I was not only treated as a subordinate, but expected to fail. The secretary I had replaced, who was in charge of training me, told me through jabbing remarks that I'd be overwhelmed, that I would not be paid well, and that equipment I had to work with was outdated and insufficient. "You'll get used to this horrible desk," she said, "and this crappy 1983 computer, and these are some projects that I never got around to doing. They're your problem now." When my first paycheck arrived she handed it to me like she was touching a paperthing turd. "Here's your paycheck," she said — "you won't be making very much money."

I answered phones for six lawyers, handled accounts payable and receivable, mail, supplies, court dockets, answered the door and greeted people, did general secretarial support as well as specialized legal support and juggled legal personalities. I had no legal training. If I seem naive for not walking out after the first week, it's because I had no frame of reference, it was my first real office job.

At the insurance company I had my own phone line, my own voice mail, and I didn't have to answer anyone else's phone. There was a giant cafeteria on the first floor building. I got paid more than I had at the law office, I had my own full color computer with games installed on it, my own work area, and the coffee was free. I thought I was in heaven. My duties were minimal: type a few memos, get the mail, make copies, arrange meetings and order refreshments for them. This was a fucking breeze; I could live like this.

The third day I was there, I was invited to join the Marketing team for their department meeting. I looked around the room and noticed that all 8 of us were women, and 3 were pregnant. This is a really progressive company, I thought. I was bewildered and flattered that I was considered important enough to have an opinion, and to join in on this meeting. Out of habit, I barely spoke. I was introduced to a round of smiles and "welcome"s. You could have dipped me in sugar I was so happy.

After a couple of weeks, my work schedule went something like this: I arrived at 8:30, turned on my computer, changed my outgoing voicemail message, got some coffee, said good morning to everyone, and played Windows Solitaire until 9:30. Then I walked over to the next cubicle and chatted with my neighbors Diane and Lori for about an hour. Sometimes Jane, who made involuntary bird noises from her cubicle and had a thing for Brain Dennehy, and Kathy, who was six months pregnant, would join us. Then my boss, who was also pregnant, gave me some eight-line memo for me to type up and distribute, and I got the mail while I was in the copy room. Then I played Windows Solitaire until lunch, went to the cafeteria and got something to bring back upstairs, sat in the lunchroom for about an hour and heard the company gossip. After that there was this computer game that involved removing stacked tile with Chinese characters on them one by one until all that was left was a computer animated dragon, more solitaire, call my mother at work and see how she was doing, call my sister at work, check the mail again, fax my friends in Chicago, get some more coffee, chat with my neighbors until 4:30, get on my bus and go home.

A couple of more weeks of this, and I was dead bored. Sure this was fabulous compared to my last job, but why did they hire me at all? I began pestering my neighbor Lori more and more. It was like summer camp. I would call her just for the fun of it, even though we could clearly hear each other through the cubicle walls. As time went on we got sillier and sillier. I created fake products for her to market using Windows Powerpoint. A big hit was a dishwashing lotion that I named "Chicken Boy." "*So tasty,*" the byline went, "*you won't believe it's a dish detergent. Sprinkle some on your favorite salad.*" Another was, "*Chicken Hawk denture cleanser, makes a lovely pasty filling.*" I grew restless sitting all day, and began a morning ritual: a little something called, "The Pulp Fiction Dance." This involved going over to Diane and Lori's cubicle, reciting honeybunny's line: "*Any of you fucking pigs move, and I'll execute every mother fucking one of you*" and doing a little impromptu Ed Grimley-esque dance while singing the music that plays during the opening credits of Pulp Fiction. Sometimes I called Lori and whispered, "*two hours and thirty two minutes to go.*" *Click.* Other times I sabotaged her screen saver and created floating banner slogans that said things like, "*I'd rather be having root canal.*"

Then there was Dave, who worked on the other side of my cubicle. Our cubicles were set up buddy-style; there was one entrance for two cubicles, one on the left and one on the right. He wasn't from our department, but because of space restraints, he was stuck with the cube across from me. He strutted around the department like a proud peacock among us womenfolk, wore way too much mousse, on casual Fridays came in wearing a tailored leather jacket, and drove a flashy sports car. All day he made grand demonstrations of how much work he had to do, and how stressed he was. His usual display was to sigh loudly, walk in a small circle, look at a piece of paper he had on the wall of his cube with lots of numbers on it, and rub his temples. He kept a picture of his bleach blonde, poor man's Pamela Sue Anderson girlfriend on his desk. Her name was Twinky or something. When he wasn't flirting with the girls in marketing, or pretending to be stressed, I was subjected to their cheesepuff conversations, which ranged from "*I miss you cupcake*" to "*Oh baby, you're getting me hot.*" Lori, Diane and I had lots of fun gossiping about Dave.

As much fun as all this was, eventually I came to this epiphany: I was getting paid to waste my life. By doing this all day long, I had lost all drive to pursue anything fruitful or interesting. It was as if someone said to me: "Go sit in that corner for an hour, don't do anything, and I'll be back with ten bucks," and repeated this hourly, and then asked me to come back the next day for more of the same. I grew to dread coming to work, because I knew there wouldn't be any work for me to do. I began volunteering to pick up overflow work from other departments. I announced at department meetings that I was available for extra projects that needed help.

That's when I started picking up on the fact that this wasn't necessarily a good thing to do. Sure, I was helping out and making myself useful, but the department was already in trouble for being lackadaisical, and I was promoting the image of the marketing department being a bunch of no good, lay-abouts. There had been so many cutbacks in the proceeding months, that almost all the marketing department projects had been turned down, resulting in an entire sedentary department.

I began to lose motivation. I scheduled dental appointments during work hours so I wouldn't have to be there all the time. I slacked off on the few tasks that I had, and let them pile up. On several mornings, Lori and I left messages on each other's voice mail saying we would be late.

One day, my boss told me my assignment would soon be over. Later that afternoon my agency called and told me this would be my last day. I packed my things, said my goodbyes, got on my bus, and went home. Not long afterward, people began quitting, getting fired, and going on maternity leave. Most of the people I worked with are now gone. They asked me back as a temp a couple of times, but I turned them down, knowing the special kind of boredom I was avoiding. I still keep in touch with Lori, who has since gotten married and has moved on to other work.

JESSICA, FUTURE KING OF THE WORLD, COHEN

Temp Time Frame

Hiya ... I write to you from the receptionist's desk of an executive search-firm on Madison Avenue. This is a heinous job. The phone system is completely fucked — and it has a nifty feature called "whisper page." You break in on the harried exec's phone conversation and you tell them they have another call. Then you have to read and interpret their subtle response, which, sometimes is nothing at all. You're lucky if they grunt at you. This interpretive exercise needs to take place in the span of 1.5 seconds. They have nothing written down about how to work the thing. Plus all the guys have names like "Joe" or "John" or "Bill" or "Jack" (I do not exaggerate). So I'm like, "Okay, they're all suits, so they all look alike to me ... Bill's the fat guy with the attitude problem, John's the bald one with stupid jokes. When the agency first offered me the job, they said, "All we have is a receptionist for $9 an hour" (as opposed to computer work for $12-15) and I was like "All right." The first thing the suits want to know when I get there is, "Can you do Microsoft Word?" I was vague, thinking they are going to make me word-process. I'm going to make sure I get more money. But then it became a moot point because the phone started ringing off the hook. The big cheese got miffed because I didn't figure the shit out instantly. The guy who trained me is Chinese, which doesn't help matters. Big language barrier. Here in New York, white guys run the show, Asians deal the technology, black guys work the mail room (which of course involves cleaning and other low grunt work) and girls answer the phone.

The desk is covered with "motivational phrases" such as "Strive to exceed your expectations." , "Rise every time you fall." I wonder if the regular receptionist has put them there for herself, if the execs put them there for her, or if someone has put them there to keep the temps stoked up. "See life as a daring adventure." Just when you think you've had enough, the computer screen saver kicks in.

Work!

Work!

"Power lies in the application of knowledge, not the knowledge itself" rolls across the screen every half second. Really makes you think, doesn't it?

I'm on my lunch break. Here at the "Everything Bagel Deli," they have figured out that I like pasta. They give me a deal. Yesterday it was Tetrazinni (chicken, fettucini, parmesan). Today it's pesto. The deal is, they give me what has to be almost a full portion for less than half price. Don't ask me why they do this. It started on Monday; they tried to sell me a pasta thing and I squinted at the price. The guy says, "Don't worry, I'll give you a small amount." He reaches first for the small plate. Then he says, "Nah." Gets a big plate, fills it up and gives me a big piece of french bread. It's more than I can eat. To the cash register guy he says, "$2.50." This raises an eyebrow, looks like it might even start a fight, but doesn't. Today, one of the guys picked up a big bottle of hot sauce which had about an inch in it and said to it, "Tomorrow, you're finished." How did I ever live anywhere but in New York?

I've learned that if I really want to make it as execu-white-chick, I'll have to start treating bike messengers and delivery guys like a lower life-form. I guess I'm a hopeless case, because I refuse. I've been instructed to decline their requests to use the bathroom, and to "watch them." I'm seized with an urge to rip the computer out of the wall, hand it to them, and say, "Run!

Run!" Because these guys really work. Especially the messengers. The execs are bursting blood vessels over some wheeling and dealing on the damn phone. They wouldn't last a day on a bike in New York. You can tell the messengers are used to being handled with suspicion; they always seem shocked when I embark on even the most innocuous conversation with them. Twice since I've started temping, a situation has arisen in which a package was lost. In both cases, the assumption was instantly made that the messenger stole it. In both cases, the (white) exec had the gall to accuse the (black) messenger immediately, and report the "theft" to the dispatcher. In both cases, the package was recovered and the messenger was innocent.

Furthermore, the execs not only don't apologize, but continue to assume that they're right somehow. Where do they get off? I want them all to get on a bike in a damn ice storm and deliver some fucking useless computer-generated mumbo jumbo to some other worthless creep across town.

Today there is a massive snowstorm. Miraculously, I go to work on time. The Chinese guy who trained me on the phone system ("Steve," not his real name; he gets mail addressed to his Chinese name) was late. I said, "Where do you come from?" expecting an answer like "Brooklyn." He said, "Hong Kong." I loved that.

I hope the unfortunate chick who endures this torture on a full-time basis recovers from her illness soon. My

tolerance is getting low. These old suits storm out to the desk to get a fax, and if the machine is out of paper, they flip out at me, demanding to know where the fax paper is kept. What I want to say is, "How the hell should I know? You work here. I'm just passing through, Big Daddy." Meanwhile, I'm juggling eight high-maintenance lines (screening calls for eight people). Because I'm a good girl and I don't speak my mind, I put all the desperate callers on hold, turn my head 45 degrees to the right, and say something like, "Why don't you check the supply closet."

I'm getting used to the phone system. I must be doing all right because there was a day last week when I couldn't work and the agency sent someone else. The next day they asked to have me back. My biggest problem is car phones and cell phones, because sometimes it's hard to hear people and then they get all bent if you ask them to repeat something. They say, "I'm on a car phone." What do they want, a medal? The other problem I have is that just about once a day someone calls and rudely asks "Who's this?" and I say, politely, "My name is Leah. I'm just filling in today" which is my code term for the dreaded slur, "temp." Alas, the response is, "Oh you're (just) a temp? Forget it." Click.

One really great thing that has come out of all this is that I've been cured of a certain kind of envy. I used to think it might be really great to have a wicked high-paying job and make a ton of money. Not anymore. These people are 100 times more miserable than any low-wage shit worker I have ever met. They have to work so fucking hard to maintain this ridiculous lifestyle they've attained, and I'm not even talking about their jobs. They have houses in the suburbs and nice cars. They have to sit in traffic in their nice cars to get to and from their suburbs countless times a year, while talking on the phone. They have nannies to hire and fire. They have way too much dry cleaning. They have summer houses to maintain, and dismal social lives. They have all kinds of stress-related illness. They have to go to some horrible over-priced gym four times a week because they sit on their asses most of the time, and if they didn't work out they'd probably become fatally constipated. They're always on the verge of hysteria. You know I'm not religious, but the word "Godless" springs to mind. I'll take my rice and beans, my 10 minute subway ride, and my roach infested Hell's Kitchen apartment any day. I wouldn't live like those people for all the money in the world.

LEAH RYAN

The Badge

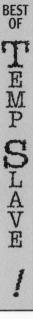

This is an actual photo of me wearing my daily garb from a temp assignment at a large computer consulting firm in Washington, DC. As a temp, I was REQUIRED to wear this humiliating badge at all times while on the job. I can still hear the snickers I would get when walking into a conference room full of company suits. Equally bad were the condescending glances from the other employees. The "contractors" had to wear badges, too, but at least theirs said "Contractor," which was a bit more dignified. If it's hard enough to blend in and be part of the office as a temp, this badge ensured the impossibility of that. Any employee caught not wearing his/her Temporary badge was reprimanded publicly, and repeat offenses were considered grounds for firing. They said the badges were needed as a security precaution, but since the full-time employees didn't wear a badge saying "Full Time," I don't get it.

Existentially, it was kind of interesting to walk around all day labeled "Temporary;" in the grand scheme of things, aren't we all?

MALCOLM RIVIERA

133

Santa is a
Temp Ho Ho Ho

My older sister was a Kelly girl. That's the closest thing I ever saw to temp employment until I was a twenty-one years old, trying to make it on my own. And not doing too well at it.

For a while, I tried to be a "bookkeeper" at a large grocery store — I counted down register drawers — but I wasn't so good at that, so they fired me. Then I fell back on telephone solicitation ("You've just won an excellent free prize."), but I wound up calling my employer an asshole and walking out.

Just before Christmas is not a good time to be jobless, because every business in town has already filled up its slots by mid-November. The shelves are full, so to speak. So I hunched my shoulders and turned up my collar and went into Western Temp Services to beg for a job. After I passed all the idiot tests, I was interviewed by a Yuppie.

"Do you know how to run a floor buffer?" he asked. I said I did not.

"That's the wrong answer," he smiled, making me wonder if this was in fact another idiot test. I looked at him the way a curious dog looks through a chain link fence.

"You should have said, 'It's been awhile since I've run one, but I think I can figure it out,' or something like that." So much for the first amendment.

"We'll call you," he said. I went home and got drunk, dreading the factory job I certainly knew was waiting for me.

At eight o' clock sharp the next morning, the phone rang. I tried not to sound like I was sleepy, but some things you just can't pull off. The girl on the phone said, "Sorry to wake you up. How do you feel about Santa Claus?"

I replied, "What," which is what I usually say when I talk to these temp people.

"Santa Claus. You know, at the mall. Santa Claus."

"You want me to be Santa Claus?" A mental picture tried to form in the pool of my mind's eye, but there were

Work!

Work!

Work!

too many ripples. Couldn't see it at all. "How much does Santa Claus make?" I asked.

"$5.25 an hour."

I said, as best as I knew how, "Ho ho ho."

By God, I looked like the old man in the sleigh. In my big red suit, with my own glasses perched above the flowing white beard, long white hair streaming behind me, I strode down the main aisle of the Southland Mall. How could they have known? The parents lined up their children at my feet and had them beg to me.

"I want a Nintendo."

"Okay," I said.

"And a mountain bike."

"You got it," I replied cheerfully. "Ho ho ho." And the child's parents would look at me like I was crazy and walk away.

Next!

When it slowed down a little, an old man on the bench near my little elf-cluttered stage told me, "This goddamn mall is useless. They should just fill it up two-feet deep with sheepshit and throw seed on it. It's goddamn useless."

"What are you doing here?" I asked him. He did not reply.

A pair of scruffy teenagers walked up to me, long hair and red eyes, and asked, "Hey, Santa, you got a joint for me for Christmas? Ha ha ha." I yanked my fake beard down and said, "Santa ain't got no joint for you kid. Santa gotta save some for himself."

MERRY CHRISTMAS FROM THE TEMP INDUSTRY!

SANTA, IT'S DECEMBER 25TH. YOU'RE FIRED!

A thirty-something woman climbed on my lap, probably thinking I was a limp old man, and purred, "What does Santa want for Christmas?" I grabbed her with both hands and said, "Santa gets off at eight."

A teenage girl, who apparently was a non-believer, began to argue with me about my identity. "You're not Santa Claus," she said, defiantly kicking aside one of her childhood building blocks.

"Sure I am. You wanna see my red nosed reindeer?" For the sake of professionalism, I added, "Ho ho ho."

I had been warned by the girl at Western Temps that little kids might puke on me, or pee on me, or worse. But none of that stuff ever happened. Being Santa Claus was perhaps the most rewarding job I will ever have held. This was the clincher: A little girl, just barely over toddlerism, hopped onto my knee and told me everything she wanted. She went on and on, and I couldn't make out a word she was saying. I just sat there and nodded, smiling at her mother (who looked relieved to be able to let go of the kid for a moment).

With real feeling, I told her, "Well, if you're a good little girl, you'll get all that and more. Ho ho ho." I placed her back down gently, and her mother led her away. From about a hundred feet off, still held by the hand, she twisted around and stared at me, and shouted, "I LOVE YOU SANTA CLAUS."

Everyone in the mall heard it. And they all saw the old man in the red suit pulling off his glasses and mopping his dewy eyes on his fuzzy sleeves.

PAUL F. HELLER

Work!

Worker Rights for Temps!

A temp worker has little or no rights in the workplace. In essence, a temp worker is close to being a nonentity. Sadly, not much can be done to alleviate the situation. A temp worker can be moved from job to job within a workplace, even though the temp may have been told they would o only one kind of job. As for job security, obviously there is none.

The normal avenues of channeling discontent about a job are not open to temps. For example, the normal course of unionizing a workplace is out of the question. Most companies set up Human Resource departments to act as a buffer between their workers and management. If a problem arises, the Human Resource managers are summoned to sort out the mess. But, this does nothing for temps since any overt complaints about a job by a temp will more than likely result in termination. Finally, getting unemployment benefits off a temp agency is like pulling teeth. Most of the time, requests for benefits are denied.

So a temp is forced to put up and shut up or get out. However, there are a few things a temp can do to gain a semblance of power in the workplace.

First, DON'T SPEED UP! SLOW DOWN! Most of the time a temp is expected to work at the rate that a full-time worker does or faster. At first a temp may want to impress upon the fact that they are capable of doing the job. But, once this is accomplished there is no reason for a temp to continue the pace. If you are working with a group of temps, band together and SLOW DOWN your rate of work. Slowing down your work allows your assignment to linger on longer. After all, why put yourself out of work? Plus, a group of temps working together cohesively puts the company notice that people cannot be treated like slaves.

Second, NEVER rat on another temp to the bossman! Trying to put yourself above other temps is a silly and ulti-

Work! Work!

mately a hopeless thing to do. The person doing the ratting may think they are getting ahead, or think that the bossman will grant special favors, or think it will lead to a full-time job. But it seldom ever does. What it does do is divide the workforce and keep people in place. To get rid of a rat, a few simple things can be done — "lose" their paperwork (make them look bad in the eyes of the bossman), chill out the rat (do not associate with the person on break time). And never volunteer to work with a rat if two people are needed for a job. In other words, make it known that they are not wanted within your work area.

Third, GET BACK AT THE BASTARDS! If you are being treated like shit by a company give it right back. Many companies entrust you with sensitive information. Use this info, "lose" it, sabotage it. Learn your job well and take every advantage possible with it.

Finally, if you are ending an assignment and really want to mess up the works legally, there is a fun thing you can do. Start talking union to everyone in the workplace. This gives you the opportunity to file charges with the National Labor Relations Board (NLRB). The NLRB is a national governmental agency set up to broker labor disputes. Under law, a worker is allowed to organize unions in the workplace. But, even with the law, workers are still fired. However, filing charges with the NLRB is a kick in the ass to a company because it forces them to deal with investigations and endless paperwork. In the best case scenario you may win your case and receive back pay sometimes amounting to thousands of dollars. But, even if you lose you can go away happy knowing that you were an incredible pain in the ass to the corporate hacks.

In closing, a workforce divided by petty jealousies, fear and self loathing is a workforce that plays into the hands of the bosses.

DON'T MAKE IT EASY FOR THEM! THEY DON'T DESERVE IT!

KEFFO

I Don't Feel Good Today!

Hey, temp kids, isn't it fun to roll out of bed in the early morning and go to a bullshit job in a square building where everyone treats you like shit?!!! NOT!!! Wouldn't you rather be doing something better with your time? Hell, I'd rather scratch my ass than have to put up with the moron work I have to do!

The fact of the matter is, if you don't feel like going to work you shouldn't. After all, how does it benefit you anyway. Sure, you get a paycheck each week, but if you miss a day of work it's probably only going to mean maybe $35-50 on your paycheck. Do you think that amount of measly money is going to make a difference in the long run. Not likely. So CALL IN SICK.

Calling in sick is fun. It's a good thing to do and you should never feel guilty about it since the assholes who run your workplace can't really tell whether or not you are really sick. If you do call in sick, make sure it is a day when you know that the bosses are going to be short staffed! This drives them up the wall!

Even better, if you want to cause complete chaos, talk to other temps in your workplace and organize a sick in. Imagine your boss pulling his hair and screaming when he finds out that his whole group of temps isn't coming to work! Not a damn thing will be done that day. Now isn't that a gas? They treat you like shit, yet, by you simply picking up the phone you can make their lives miserable!

Need an excuse? Here are some excuses!

1) I have a cold. (Make sure to cough into the phone.)

2) My daddy died. (For the tenth time.)

3) My car won't start. (Of course it might help if you put the key into the ignition!)

4) I have a flat tire. (Not!)

5) I'm out of gas. (Not!)

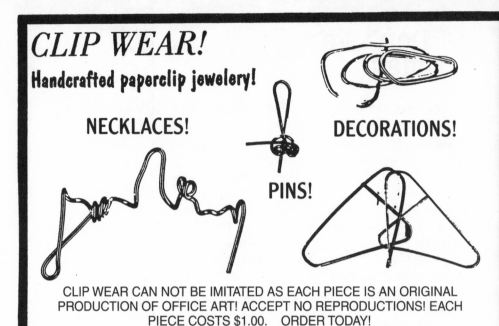
6) It's a religious holiday.

7) My mommy died. (For the ninth time.)

8) A tanker fell over on the main road.

9) My car was stolen.

10) I have a doctors appointment.

Well, those are some of the usual excuses to get out of work. How about some unusual excuses. Considering the intelligence levels of most bosses, the following excuses may very well work. So give 'em a try.

1) I have a festering pimple on my ass.

2) It's the anniversary of the invention of silly putty.

3) I drank too much last night.

4) They're showing an episode of *Gilligan's Island* where Gilligan shoots the moves on Ginger.

5) My cat has diarrhea.

6) Your breath stinks. I need a day off the clear my lungs.

7) I broke my tail bone sitting on the toilet.

8) I need a day off just to think about how much I enjoy working.

9) I don't feel like shoveling shit today.

10) It's National Sick Day for Temps. FUCK YOU!

The whole point in taking off a day of work is so you can do the kinds of things you really want to do. In fact, in my case, I'd rather go to work sick, do a half-assed job and call in sick only when I have something important planned.

So fellow temps, take a day off. It's good for you!

KEFFO

INTERVIEW: Chris Carlsson On Work, Temps, and Processed World

Chris Carlsson is one of the founding members of *Processed World.* If you don't know about *Processed World,* it is the longest running anti-work, anti-boss zine. Started in 1981, PW has been interested in how people related to their work environment, issues on technology, temp work, theory and above all humor fill the pages of this magazine. PW members used to don outlandish outfits and do street theater in the financial district of San Francisco. PW is playful and open to anyone who is pissed off, frustrated and hell bent on exposing the corporation. PW has also served as a starting point for many writers and artists including Tom Tomorrow, Angles Bocavage, Melissa Gebbie, Paul Mavrides, Jay Kinney, Dennis Hayes, Ace Backwards and JRS. And guess what, me too (#30). Despite all this PW has been criticized for not being "ist" enough. PW members while having many kinds of political connections, never aligned the collective with the various competing ideologies. This has caused a lot of confusion. No matter. PW has always been on the side of working people and always had a hopeful vision of the future. Early this year, Chris Carlsson decided to leave the PW collective to work on other projects. What he has to say about work and zines is instructive. In the years ahead, PW will be a reference point for many people interested in late 20th century work issues.

—KEFFO

KEFFO: PW is the Big Daddy of self-published work magazines. Looking back, can you tell me what self-publishing was like when the PW collective started?

CHRIS CARLSSON: In the beginning (in my apartment in SF's Haight Ashbury) we typeset PW on a Compu-writer Jr. phototypesetter, cut and paste galleys and graphics onto layout boards (heavy use of purloined corporate graphics with added captions and speech bubbles, not much "real art" except the covers), and printed in a garage in Berkeley on a Multilith 1250 press (and 4-13 members printed on an "anarchist-owned" Multilith a few blocks away at 719 Ashbury in the Haight). Then we'd run them through a folding machine and hold a "Collating Party," which we conceptualized as a kind of urban subversive barn-raising. After a beer and pot saturated day of slowly assembling magazines, we'd box 'em all up and take them to a friendly Filipino owned bindery in Oakland and he'd give us a deal on stitching and trimming, and voila! a finished magazine. Later we succumbed to the market and had the magazine printed on a web press and bound by a union printer in SF, and still later (issue 26 and on) we went to the cheap book printers in the midwest.

Distribution was a pretty straight ahead job of hustling local stores to carry it on consignment and trying to get Last Gasp to push it around the rest of country. Eventually a network of distributors and stores around the country was developed and supplied, but that took a few issues and over a year to get established. PW's "system" has since collapsed twice due to inattention from the collective and been rebuilt nearly from scratch. It's always arduous, unrewarding, difficult to collect, expensive to ship, and were it not for the exposure, sales and good mail, there wouldn't be any way to justify the hassle.

K: Your name is very recognizable with PW so your leaving the mag must have been a difficult choice. Why are you leaving?

CC: I had nothing left to do in PW. I no longer had any particular reason to participate in publishing it. I feel it has become repetitive and lacks a passionate purpose for publishing. I found the collective meetings tedious and lacking intellectual stimulation. I am dissatisfied with the critical/analytical approaches of the current crop of PWers. The fact that it remains the only forum where work is explored in some detail and commonly held in contempt is its strongest argument for continuing, but I got bored with Tails of Toil, and I am bored with the magazine format. The writing is flat and there's no edge. The graphics are less edgy and more pat and predictable. The letters from readers have dried up and the ones that do show up every few weeks are far less thoughtful. PW is not hitting nerves like it once did, and looking over the past 2 issues, perhaps the past 4 (though I'm very fond of #30) it's obvious that it's drifting and groping for a purpose as it passes through vague themes on auto-pilot. I think part of the reason is that PW has become isolated and is not connected to anything going on in the world. There's not exactly a worker's movement underway. PW missed the boat on the Internet because none of us really enjoy participating in cyberspace —

145

it's too dull, too many people running off at the mouth (no editing, eech!), too much work to wade through the billions of glowing pixels in search of some pearl of wisdom or wit. Frankly, I'd rather read a good, well-designed book or zine. Creatively, I'm deep into an experiment in interactive multimedia (what was that buzzing sound I just heard?) focused on San Francisco history — a couple of my PW colleagues are my partners in this project too.

K: Do you have any advice for people starting up their own zine?

CC: Have a passionate reason for publishing. Strive for originality and high quality writing and art. There's too much low-quality, knock-off, self-indulgent masturbatory micromedia floating around already, so don't waste your time and ours: Make it as good as you can, think about the pleasure you want to give your readers, and don't buy into this lazy anti-aesthetics crap. Figure out where the money is going to come from. Without advertising, you're probably going to be dumping serious sums into a black hole. Distribution is a lot of work and not much fun. If you plan to go for major distribution, take it seriously as a part-time job because it needs steady attention and timely work if it's going to generate any revenue at all. The best thing is to get money together some

> There's too much low-quality, knock-off, self-indulgent masturbatory micromedia floating around already . . .

other way, and make your publication very inexpensive and available through mail order, sit back and get ready for a deluge of wacky, interesting, and confusing mail. If you don't like mail, and don't really want to talk to people, it's probably stupid to publish.

K: Did PW ever consider taking ads?

CC: Not really. It came up for discussion every few years, and occasionally a hip alternative small business would offer to buy an ad, but we systematically rejected that route. Of course, there's the question of being less independent and beholden to advertisers, but realistically I doubt if we'd ever have catered to an advertiser editorially. I always felt that advertising was the antithesis of PW, and I was proud to announce during street sales, "No ads, and no religion." The impact of our anti-ads would diminish if juxtaposed to real ads. Real ads are stupid and ugly. A related question might be about whether we ever considered having a paid staff. Because if we succeeded in financing the zine with ads, we may have ended up like Maximum Rock 'n' Roll, with an annual monetary surplus to dump, or else we may have had to hire people to do the mundane tasks like mail/ check processing, banking, shipping, distribution, etc. But then why shouldn't the creative contributors be paid too?

And what about the people who came to meetings and occasionally offered a comment or criticism, sometimes influentially, should they be paid? The sudden influx of money creates an unequal hierarchy of participation, and brings up payroll taxes and all the other headaches of small business, to boot. And the problems of the magazine and the collective revolve even more completely and intensely around money. Besides, all these bad attitudes and lazy drunken people (the PW collective that is) made a terribly inefficient operation (which we did for free, anyway), so fights would have broken out over why no one was doing the work, and wages would only have complicated everything. Money sucks.

K: What does the "information highway" mean for self-publishing? And what about Big Brother butting in?

CC: There's going to be a whole lotta words being uploaded; in fact, there already are. Self-publishing will no longer pass through the filter of mustering finances, editing, design, and all the things that help make a better end result. I suspect that there will be some kind of constitutional type decision made eventually that provides for some kind of right to free speech on the net, but it wouldn't surprise me if it was proscribed into an area with a bad interface, clunky access, etc. But it's pretty much up for grabs, so who knows what'll turn out in 5 to 10 years. So far there's not much reason to be optimistic, but most attempts by central authorities to control communication eventually fail and I think the US ruling class has that one figured out. It's better for them to let you vent as much as you want, but just make sure it stays marginalized.

K: The unions are out of favor, companies are cutting back and temp work seems to be the future. Is there anything workers can do anymore?

CC: There's always a lot of vulnerable points in any modern business. Workers have some of the power they've always had, insofar as they conspire to threaten hardware, data, communications, and the things that really matter to management. Historically workers have banded together when they saw their shared predicament. That's harder these days because today's temporary and transient work life tends to mitigate against the development of self-identified communities based on work. Individuals always have a number of options for sabotage, but that's a complicated question that needs to be carefully thought through regarding the consequences of any given act. In general, sabotage rarely promotes solidarity, and has from time to time been used by provocateurs to undermine worker organizing. Nevertheless, sometimes it's all you got. Medium term, we have to develop among ourselves connections we can count on, understandings of how power works in our daily lives and how we can reduce its effect through mutual aid. A longer term strategy must address the absurd and self-destructive division of labor, ultimately we have to abolish a lot of the work we're doing now and get on with a lot of important tasks that are being ignored like the ecological holocaust. I don't think capital or the state is going to step in and facilitate this transition since it's going to over-throw their power.

K: What are people actively organizing for or against? What issues need to be addressed?

CC: Laundry lists abound. I think African-Americans are getting pretty restive, as are poor people in general. Poverty and homeless-ness, coupled with wide-spread racism, will probably lead to some serious explosions in the years to come. Expand-ing the police presence and the insane jail building and incarceration plans are clearly an unworkable solution, so some kind of deeper structural reforms can be expected from the more thoughtful elements of the ruling class. But things may have to fall apart and get a lot more expensive before such reformers have their day. I think we need to focus on developing political communities from which we can

launch visionary initiatives and protect ourselves when the shit comes down. We have to begin fleshing out the pieces of the puzzle that is our idea of the life we want to live.

K: How will work be organized by the year 2010?

CC: In my crystal ball there are millions of sweating, dark-skinned people all over the world breathing toxic fumes, drinking poisoned water, and churning out millions of cheap and useless but profitable commodities. Most are unemployed most of the time, as are the formerly privileged white folks in the north-ern latitudes. Guaran-teed payments keep most people alive but anomie is rampant. In spite of the much heralded communica-tions revolution which has swept the globe since the end of the last century, most people have more limited vocabularies, common speech is more primitive than ever, and text-based media are suffering precipitous declines in access times and distribu-tion. Work for most people is a highly controlled, extremely tiring and danger-ous activity, which would be mono-tonous if the pace were a bit slower and also if they weren't regularly laid off.

> . . . but most attempts by central authorities to con-trol communication eventually fail and I think the US ruling class has that one figured out. It's better for them to let you vent as much as you want, but just make sure it stays marginal-ized.

The creative types are encouraged to apply their skills to the demands of the marketplace, and are rewarded when successful with stock options, private homes and vehicles, and inclusion in the social clubs of the upper crust of the permanently employed. The unsuccessful are soon discarded into the lower tiers to find a "real job."

K: Well, in other words, nothing is going to change because what you describe is already happening, maybe not as dire, but still the same.

K: What are you reading these days?

CC: Really? Well, mostly history books about San Francisco, most recently stuff on the SF General Strike of 1934, the ULWU (Longshoreman's Union) and *Black San Francisco* by Allan Broussard (dry and academic, but some useful information). Occasionally a bit of science fiction. I'm reading the Susan Cooper series *The Dark Has Risen* to my daughter. On my stack is the latest Octavia Butler novel *Parable of the Sower.* I seem to read semi-regularly the *SF Chronicle, SF Weekly, SF Bay Guardian, Nation, Anderson Valley Advertiser, Wired,* *Mediamatic, Harper's,* The *New Yorker,* and probably a few others I can't remember. I never have enough time to read, but that's partly because I like basketball and baseball and I have cable TV.

K: WHAT!!! You mean you don't read Temp Slave? That sucks but I'll forgive you since I'm a sports and cable addict too. I'm not even in the closet, I'm loud and proud of my viewing habits!

K: The temp industry: suicide or subversion?

CC: Subversion. Have fun or don't bother, since whatever you do has a low probability of success. But resistance can be fun, and at least it is good practice. Otherwise, follow the American Dream and start your own business selling suicide kits to the unhappy temps you leave behind. (Order my "Make $10,000 a week in your spare time stuffing envelops" corporate seminar package for only $495.) Self-exploitation is much tidier and usually less painful than suffering someone else's capricious dictates.

The Renegade Temp

Every so often I'll discover that my resources and good fortunes are on the verge of becoming thoroughly exhausted. I know what's coming next and the anticipated horror of it usually launches me into a frenzied booze binge. Shortly thereafter, my senses dulled, my mind hopelessly muddled, I emerge from an alcoholic haze to find that I have become "employed."

To my way of thinking, there is almost nothing as humiliating as employment. To me it is synonymous with servitude and idiocy. There is something suicidal about this lemming-like desire to be employed.

But like most values the wealthy have sought to instill in the under classes — values like sobriety, fidelity and patience, all of which the wealthy steadfastly reject in practice — the veneration of full time, year round employment is something I find repulsive.

My aversion to employment doesn't spring from a privileged background. I was born into a family of lower-middle class workers, who positively worshipped employment. Like most amongst their caste, they even attached self worth to employment. The "Good Job" was the essential element to their definition of success.

Thankfully, this feeble ethic was drummed out of me early on by the tyrannical bosses who resided over the gas stations and hamburger factories of my youth. I learned more about our society during this brief period than I had in all the preceding years of classroom brainwash about the unsurpassed munificence of capitalistic exploitation.

What I learned is that employment is a form of controlled dying. I learned that employment amounted to individuals selling off large portions of their lives to soulless thugs who, in the name of profit, will perform on those isolated parcels of life whatever violence they believe is

most lucrative. And like any other parasite, the employer will continually demand more until the host has been sucked dry, at which time the leached tissue is left to putrefy as the hunt for fresh meat begins.

Unable to escape this morbid predicament entirely, I've opted for what I believe is the next best solution — I participate in it as little as possible.

Over the past 15 years I've never been employed for more than 7 months during any single year. My most successful year to date was 1989 when I used a fake resume to land a job as an executive manager for Kohl's Department Stores. That year I worked a total of 3 months and earned nearly $10,000 before being fired for what they said was my gross incompetence. I didn't bother to point out that the 3 months it took them to discover I was a complete fraud — when I was doing very little to suggest otherwise — might indicate that their incompetence was somewhat more gross than my own.

Although pay is important, it is certainly secondary. Easy employment is the top priority. I'll take an easy job that pays $5 an hour over an ass grinder that pays $6 any day. In most circumstances, however, there is little correlation between pay and the amount of work being done. In a system as thoroughly fucked as ours, that sort of consistency just isn't to be expected.

You might think it would be difficult finding work with an employment history like mine. Over the past 15 years I've been fired from 30 jobs. Most of the time, I have no problem becoming unemployed. For one thing, my standards are unbelievably low. Unless I notice an opportunity to bluff my way into some soft middle-management position, I make it a habit to shoot for jobs that have no prestige. The jobs that offer no chance for advancement. The jobs others are embarrassed by. In a pinch, I'll even take a job requiring hard work. Of course, I'll probably do little more than stand around and drink coffee until I'm fired, but I'll take it.

Another reason I have few problems finding employment is that I am an accomplished liar when it comes to job applications and resumes. Is there really a law requiring me to be truthful? I suppose there may be, but I hardly fucking care.

My special spiel is that I've just been laid off from a job that I've held for 13 years. I'll say the factory moved south — Mexico, maybe — or that it was sold off in pieces after the corporation that bought it was bought out. More importantly, I'll tell them my job title was something like "Bottle Cap Assembler" or "Label Pasting Operator" and add that I never made more than $6 an hour.

This implies three things to the employer:

1) That I am loyal to the core to any creep willing to hire me on, 2) I have an incredibly high tolerance for

mundane, soul-crushing work and 3) I am a goddamned idiot who knows absolutely nothing about the value of money. Not coincidentally, these are the three qualities employers love above all others.

The interview is even easier. As I mentioned earlier, my job searches are usually performed while suffering from some form of alcoholic sickness, so appearing subnormal and docile isn't much of a stretch. And since the person doing the interview is usually just a little bit stupid, I don't need to appear all that convincing. As I enter the room, I make sure to hand them my long list of bogus references. If the quisling should bother to check any of them out he or she will have every lie I tell them confirmed. My friends tend to be fuckers, too.

So I get hired. It is always a disheartening experience. Whether you're a french fry inspector or an assistant director of marketing. Not surprisingly, there are breeds that enjoy the experience. (And there are people who find the taste of human shit sexually exciting.) The worst of this lot are the miscreants who claim to love their work. I don't doubt them. A lot of people loved Hitler too. In the world of slavery, loving the master has always been a form of psychic defense. It's not uncommon for the condemned to develop a love of their executioner.

I've also noticed that there is no real difference between the supposedly "good" jobs I've scammed my way into and the shit jobs, which are my bread and butter. Eventually it all comes down to petty squabbles and meaningless drudgery. The "higher up" positions tend to be dominated by a more aggressive form of ignorant, but the degree of their ignorance is no less severe.

Not that I'm any kind of fucking proletariat exemplar. I may very well be the worlds worst employee. My ability to produce begins going to hell after about two weeks. If I haven't figured out some sort of plan for shirking the bulk of my responsibilities within that time, then basically I'll just sit around drinking coffee and reading newspapers until someone takes it upon themselves to fire me.

The companies without the foresight to unload me in the beginning usually come to regret it. The longer

> What I learned is that employment is a form of controlled dying. I learned that employment amounted to individuals selling off large portions of their lives to soulless thugs who, in the name of profit, will perform on those isolated parcels of life whatever violence they believe is most lucrative. And like any other parasite, the employer will continually demand more until the host has been sucked dry, at which time the leached tissue is left to putrefy as the hunt for fresh meat begins.

I'm employed, the more resentful I tend to become. If I'm employed long enough to become eligible for unemployment benefits, my general disposition tends to worsen considerably. I become all elbows and thumbs. Everything I touch seems to either breakdown or malfunction. I begin suffering from an amalgamation of mental disorders. A strange hybrid of narcolepsy and Tourette's syndrome overcomes me. When not dozing, it becomes nearly impossible for me to address a boss or select coworkers as anything other than "Fuckface." When feeling especially piqued, I'll appear for work dressed in a school - girl's uniform or as an extraordinarily hairy and flabby belly dancer. In this guise I like to adorn my rather large navel with an over-ripe plum.

Still, I don't get fired as often as you would expect. Then of course, I have to quit. But I'd rather be fired. It's more fun and usually more interesting. And much more satisfying. Some places just won't fire you though. So when this happens I try to set a goal for myself and when I accomplish it I promptly quit. For quite a while my goal was to perform some act of sabotage or theft. Like stealing a forklift and driving it off a ledge into a river or using the company letterhead to inform all important clients that they should go fuck themselves.

Lately though, my favored pre-exit goal is getting someone fired. But not just any poor slob. I try to get the biggest bastard possible. My favorite targets are mid-level managers. Ones who will screw anybody in order to enhance their own standing. And as they are often of low intelligence and highly paranoid, they tend to be vulnerable.

A few well placed phone calls will usually get the job done. Several calls to the wife of the manager's boss will often do the trick. First, I identify myself as my mark and then tell her how much I'd love to fuck her fat ass. It's really that easy.

And when the axe falls, I take it as if it were a sign from the gods. I walk straight into payroll, twitching uncontrollably, I inform them I'm hearing voices telling me to do horrible things and that I think I should leave immediately. I tell them to forward my check.

Then I sprint the hell out of there.

BUCK HORN

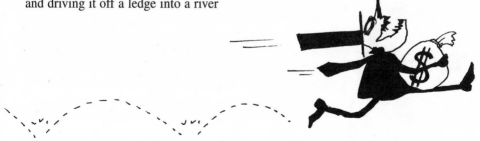

153

Life Denied

"You have all that money saved and now you're leaving the country to blow it all. You don't have anything." A FRIEND COUNSELING ME

"I never wanted anything. Not what you have anyway." MY REPLY

Some people have made it a cottage industry to describe just how rotten work is. But oftentimes they've never worked a day in their lives. Utopian alternatives are offered up as an exotic dish to be looked at but never feasted on. Most people who actually work understand this, because, with no where to turn they put their nose to the grindstone (literally) and put in their time. I am one of those people.

This doesn't make me a bad person. No political label should be applied to what I do. Because the fact of the matter is: The kind of life the prophets of the no work school only talk about is the kind of life I ache for. Every single atom in my body aches to be free. Every single second I spend working is a denial of the kind of life I really want to live. To work is to deny life.

The old saying goes, "Knowledge is Power." I beg to differ, I think the saying should go, "Knowledge is a Curse." Freedom, my definition of it anyway, is the right to have a say in the direction of your life. But, once given the knowledge of what freedom really is, things become very difficult.

I wrote of my experiences working in London in the last issue. I only told you half of the story. I didn't tell you the other part of the experience that stuck with me, that forces me to evaluate my given situation on a daily basis. I'm tormented with the knowledge, the ghosts of the experience torture me.

For six months of my adult life I had the freedom and money to do whatever the hell I wanted. (Eventually of course I ran out of money and had to work in London.) I lived on a shoestring budget and hit the road.

154

It started in Ireland. I didn't go straight to Dublin. Instead I flew into Shannon airport in the west. The west of Ireland is a desolate place and this is where my journey began.

The minute I stuck my thumb out on the road a weird kind of drama played out. Who was going to pick me up and where was I going? In the space of some people's lives they meet maybe 5 really interesting people. I can truthfully say that I met 10 interesting people everyday. Waves and waves of people with their own quirks, political statements, family stories, prejudices. It was like a flash, boom, there they are, there they aren't.

I found myself becoming a chameleon, adapting myself to the situation at hand. Hilarious and sometimes unnerving scenarios occurred.

Boom. I'm walking on a lonely hilly country road five miles out of the town of Dingle in County Kerry. I was on my way to a town called Ballyferriter. On the walk, I noticed a hard scrabble offshoot of a road that led into the hills. I decided to follow it. Around the bend sat a row of thatched roof shanties. Suddenly, a filthy looking old man walked out from behind one of the houses and began gibbering at me in Irish. I threw my hands up and tried to explain that I didn't speak the language. He stopped and looked at me, not just looked, he did an x-ray number on me from head to toe. He walked a full circle around me with his head moving up and down. I suppose I looked like an alien dropped from a space ship. He began laughing at me so hard that huge gobs of green and yellow snot dripped out of his nose.

Boom. I took a ferry to the Blasket Islands, the furthermost western island group off the mainland of Ireland. The natives call it the last parish before America. At one time it was a thriving Irish community but the harsh conditions and the lure of the mainland led to its' demise. The ferry boat captain took a liking to me and allowed me to stay in a house he owned on the island. There were about 5 other people on the whole island. What was meant to be a 4 day drip turned into three and a half weeks. The island was 2 miles long and 1 mile wide and every part of it had a history. I spent my time hiking, thinking and often times cliff climbed buck naked for hours on end. Day trippers from other countries visited. At nights we sat around a peat fire, told stories or sang songs. Other nights I sat on the northern cliffs of the island and watched the sun go down. Unlike my life in America, I'd have to say that every single day was meaningful on the Blasket Island.

Boom. I was in County Clare. I sat down on the edge of the Cliffs of Moher, the steepest cliffs in all of Europe. The waves of the Atlantic Ocean crashed into the rocks making a thunderous sound. A group of German motorcycle punks were nearby, running around, laughing and yelling. They came over to me and we all looked over the cliffs. Not a word was exchanged but I looked at their eyes and I saw gears shifting inside their brains. I understood.

Boom. I arrived late at a hostel in Galway. The owner informed me that they only had one bed available. I agreed to take it. I pulled off my clothing and climbed into the top bunk bed and fell fast asleep. The next morning I woke up to see 15 sets of naked breasts staring me in the face. The owner had given me a bed in the women's sleeping quarter. I smiled.

Boom. I was in the Burren. The Burren is a wildlife area in County Galway that's been touched by glaciers. I walked for what seemed like endless miles through thickets of brush. I came up over a hill and was amazed to discover an area of land that looked like a meteor had hit it. Slate rocks with deep gouges were everywhere. A herd of feral goats stood at one end of the rocks. They stared at me for a few seconds and then ran away.

Boom. It was a late afternoon and I was sitting up against a bombed out building in the Bogside neighborhood of Derry, N. Ireland. A mouse like man approached me and started giving me shit. "The boys want to knew who the fuck you are. Are you SAS (British Special Air Services) or CIA?" I told him I was just hanging out. "Well, people just don't hang out here. Take a look at the walls up there," he said while pointing. He was referring to the huge stone walls that encircle the main shopping area of Derry. "Why don't you smile, because the Brits are taking your picture," he said. Sure enough, I craned my neck and saw a person inside a tower aiming a camera at me. The man asked me where I was staying and I told him. That night another man knocked on my door and asked if I had ordered a taxi. He looked at me from head to toe with a grim look on his face. If he was a taxi driver well then, I'm the Pope. He wasn't a taxi driver. Early the next day, I went back to the Bogside and was buzzed into the offices of Sinn Fein (the political wing of the IRA) to meet "the boys."

These stories are just a few of the chance meetings and situations I found myself in.

Internally things were percolating. I hadn't seen a TV in months and I no longer cared. It amazed me to discover just how much more my synapses were firing. The road life toughened me up. Muscles sprouted and the harsh wind

> I threw my hands up and tried to explain that I didn't speak the language. He stopped and looked at me, not just looked, he did an x-ray number on me from head to toe. He walked a full circle around me with his head moving up and down. I suppose I looked like an alien dropped from a space ship. He began laughing at me so hard that huge gobs of green and yellow snot dripped out of his nose.

put a burn on my face making me look like the healthiest person you'd ever want to meet. It was pure joy. It was a complete disconnection from the slop that had been fed into my brain while living in America. Once, while crossing a bridge, I took out my clothing and threw it over the side. From there on in I lived as close to the land as I could.

You see, when I tell you via the pages of TS! that I hate work, I really mean it. I know the other side of life. I didn't have to read it in a book. The bosses also know the other side of life, thus, it's their imperative to make sure you spend your days toiling at meaningless jobs. Your work and mine, finances their acquisition of the good life. Bill Gates blathers on and on about his new dream home. How did he afford it? Donnie Trump buys another office building. Donnie Trump buys a city block. How did he afford it? Well, friends, we bought it for him. He went to a bank and got a loan. Who put the money in the bank to begin with? Who toiled to make the wealth of this country possible? We do the work and they take the vacations.

Trust me, just this once. Given the opportunity to witness and experience the magic and beauty of this world you'll never want to work another day in your life. If you work and you work hard, you can intellectualize various reasons as to why you work. Maybe it's an ingrained ethic. Maybe you believe that what you do is important. Maybe you do it to make Mommy and Daddy proud of you. Maybe you don't know better.

When I step out of my apartment and head off to work I feel a shortness of breath as if someone is standing and stomping on my chest. As I drive away, I look at the stressed-out faces of the other people around me. I look at myself in the mirror and know that I too have made a pact with the devil. One more day of work. One more day of denial.

KEFFO

Working Poor

By now you've pushed your way past the panhandlers, the gutter punks, the rag-wearing lunatics waving their arms and ranting on the street corner, the vent sitters, the cardboard box residents, the lines at feeding stations, the food-coupon users in front of you at the grocery store, the ill-clad families cluttering up your perfect little world, the stinking fetid trashy humanoids that live in their cars. You look at them and detest them. You look at them and you see yourself if payday never arrives at the end of the week. You're one week away from the street. You're better than them, though. You close your eyes.

I think about food, hunger and poverty. Being poor sucks.

I was born the son of sharecroppers. No, wait a minute, I was so poor that I had to walk 10 miles to school in bare feet. No, that's not right, either. My family was so poor that they thought a bun, a hot dog, and mustard was a three course dinner. Oh what the hell, it wasn't anything like that. I must be thinking of someone else's life.

But let me tell you, the wolves have knocked on the door. Sometimes too close for comfort. There are only been a few times when I thought I had reached an end, the point where you wither and hang on for dear life to fight with a student loan that just came in the mail. I asked Daddy to tide me over until the money came. He laughed in my face and told me that I had made my bed and now I should sleep in it. The first week of poverty wasn't so bad: I ate lentil soup for breakfast, lunch and dinner. The second week it was peanut butter, white bread and water. The third week was the killer. I couldn't find a crumb to get caught in my teeth, a salt patch to lick, or anything else for that matter. I didn't eat for four days out of that week. My pants started sagging on my body. I found some clothesline and used it as a belt. I walked around like a latter day Jethro Bodean, blue jeans and white rope belt. The fourth week, I put on a long coat that reached to my knees. I walked to the nearest grocery store and stuffed the coat full of anything

Work!

Work!

Work!

I could get my hands on. At that point, I didn't give a damn if I was caught. Luckily, I absconded with my ill begotten goods and in an insane feeding frenzy gorged myself into a food coma. Finally, the check arrived and I could live again.

The other time, I was in London. I had arrived from Amsterdam with one pound in my pocket. I wasn't able to work until the following week, and I had nowhere to stay. I wandered around for hours, past restaurants filled with people shoveling food in their mouths, past bars with people guzzling brew. The night grew longer. Feeling completely defeated, I found a doorway and collapsed in a heap. People walked by and stared at me. I knew what they were thinking. I was a loser, a bum. The sight of me scared them. I lasted out the night. The very next day I swallowed my pride and called my grandparents and asked them to wire me some money immediately. In the meantime, while I waited, I went to bars in Euston Square and talked an Australian girl into letting me sleep on her floor. She agreed and offered her bed. Little did she know I was just going to sleep in her bed because the brutal act of survival had tapped any energy I had.

I've never forgotten those incidents. I'm a poor touch for panhandlers. People think I'm naive when I give them money. I know better. Anyway, ever since then, I've dodged the bogeyman of poverty by keeping a job or jobs just to keep going. But there's always the gnawing feeling that it's going to end the next week or the week after.

There are degrees of poorness. Having some money means you can have some things. Having no money means you can have nothing. A nest egg is built. Your car breaks down, you become ill, the nest egg is gone. There's no shame in being poor. But, it is shameful if your mind is poor. It doesn't mean that you have to be stupid.

I'm always interested in the perception of the poor by the people who have.

A co-worker once told me about life growing up dirt-poor on a Wisconsin farm. He wanted to go to a school function but the price of admission was a donation of canned food that would be given to poor people. He searched the empty cupboards and found a can of beans and a can of dog food. He deftly took the label off the beans and switched it with the can of dog food. He laughed while telling me this story, imagining the look of horror and curiosity on the face of the poor shithead who eventually opened the can. I laughed, too, thinking how appropriate it symbolized America — a nice facade and a lump of poo inside. I've got a dollar, you have nothing, I'm better than you.

One night a woman in a bar in Madison, Wisconsin, sent me a drink. Against my better judgement, I decided to walk over and talk with her. She was Native American. She told me she had lived in a car with her child in Chicago and had finally moved to Madison. She was now a high-priced call girl servicing the political, business and academic elites of Madison. As she told it, although Madison is small, the population has its kinks. She wasn't trying to pick me up for a "date;" she just wanted some company. She began bragging to me about the thousands of dollars she makes a week at her job. I asked her about being poor. "Fuck it," she said. I asked her about her tribe on the reservation. "Fuck 'em," she told me. "Anyone too stupid to try to make an effort deserves to be poor. Look at me, look how far I've come. If I can do it, anyone can do it. I have a brand new car. I have $400 shoes. I buy anything I want." I was totally awed by this Hiawatha Alger story of a successful business woman in America. Upside-down, right-side-up, even call girls are pointing fingers.

For the life of me I couldn't understand how it came to be that I was hired. In my wildest thoughts, I imagined a human resource person sitting at his desk, bored out of his skull, looking at the sloppily written applications. He was drunk, his pants were at his ankles, and he was wanking himself. Finally, he threw his hands in the air, sighed once or twice, spread the applications out on the desk, closed his eyes and pointed to an application bearing my name. Thus, I was hired.

A strange thing happened to me about a year and a half ago. In the middle of yet another temp job, a company called me and offered me a real job. Good money, health benefits from day one — I couldn't refuse it.

I thought I had hit the motherlode that I was on a path to easy street. I eagerly assumed my new occupation and dreamed of better days. But, it never really ends does it? Life is still a continual nightmare of fears, worries and inertia.

A relationship ended and I moved to the low-rent district of Madison. Wild raccoons roam in the backyard of my apartment building eating out of trash cans. I come home from work and a coon with an ass as big as my own ambles up to my car to greet me. Only when I pick up a stick and wave it does the raccoon realize that I am not HIS pet. It runs up a tree next to the entrance of the house and growls at me.

The people who share the building are a cross between Herman Munster and Howard Hughes. So dirt poor that they bum money from me in the hallways. So disconnected from the fabric of everyday life that they think junk mail is like gold. One guy spends his time looking out of his peephole waiting for me to leave my apartment just so he can open his door and talk to me. Other times he stands in front of the building listening to his police scanner and looking up and down the street. Another guy, the prototypical forgotten man, tenses when he sees me and runs into his apartment, locking his doors as quickly as he can.

I have the job but I can't have a life. That's how it goes. The job provides a roof over my head. The job steals my time, making it impossible for me to experience adventure. The job puts money in my pocket. I put the money in someone else's pocket. I move forward and money starts flowing into my bank account. I feel contented. I walk out of my apartment and run full force into piss, shit and stasis. I enrich myself and my life becomes poorer as a result. No matter how you look at it, I'm still poor, poor, poor.

One day, I volunteered through my company to work at a local food bank. A gymnasium filled with neatly stacked and sorted boxes greeted me. I walked through the aisles licking my lips, staring longingly at the morsels. It was like being Homer Simpson dancing through a room full of doughnuts, only I wasn't allowed to have anything. I moved boxes of food around, some wise asses had donated liver pate and cans of truffles. I wondered what the person who got the truffles would think they were. The person would probably think it was dog food! I mean shit, I've never even tasted them before. All the food taunted me, ridiculed me, I wanted a payback at that food. I wanted to eat that food. I was going to steal some of the food. I caught myself. I was just dreaming. I walked away. I went home to the bare cupboards and the raccoons.

Hell is a dark doorway. Hell is heaping endless bowls of lentil soup. Hell is a gymnasium full of food. Hell is temp work. Hell is any work. Hell is my hunger. And hell is your pompous, self satisfied shit eating grin on your bloated hipster face.

KEFFO

A MESSAGE FROM MANAGEMENT
WILL THE LAST WORKER FIRED
FROM THEIR JOB, PLEASE TURN
OUT THE LIGHTS, AND TAKE
OUT THE GARBAGE.